Practice the TABE®!

Test of Adult Basic Education

Practice Test Questions

D1536822

Published by

Complete TEST
Preparation Inc.

ISBN-13: 978-1928077374 (Complete Test Preparation Inc.)
ISBN-10: 1928077374

Version 6.2 January 2015

Published by
Complete Test Preparation Inc.
921 Foul Bay Rd.
Victoria BC Canada V8S 4H9
Visit us on the web at http://www.test-preparation.ca
Printed in the USA

About Complete Test Preparation Inc.

The Complete Test Preparation Inc. Team has been publishing high quality study materials since 2005. Thousands of students visit our websites every year, and thousands of students, teachers and parents all over the world have purchased our teaching materials, curriculum, study guides and practice tests.

Complete Test Preparation Inc. is committed to providing students with the best study materials and practice tests available on the market. Members of our team combine years of teaching experience, with experienced writers and editors, all with advanced degrees.

Team Members for this publication

Editor: Brian Stocker MA
Contributor: Dr. C. Gregory
Contributor: Dr. G. A. Stocker DDS
Contributor: D. A. Stocker M. Ed.
Contributor: Sheila M. Hynes, MES York, BA (Hons)

Find us on Facebook

www.facebook.com/CompleteTestPreparation

Contents

Getting Started

ONGRATULATIONS! By deciding to take the Test of Adult Basic Education (TABE®), you have taken the first step toward a great future! Of course, there is no point in taking this important examination unless you intend to do your very best in order to earn the highest grade you possibly can. That means getting yourself organized and discovering the best approaches, methods and strategies to master the material. Yes, that will require real effort and dedication on your part but if you are willing to focus your energy and devote the study time necessary, before you know it you will be on you way to a brighter future.

We know that taking on a new endeavour can be a little scary, and it is easy to feel unsure of where to begin. That's where we come in. This study guide is designed to help you improve your test-taking skills, show you a few tricks of the trade and increase both your competency and confidence.

The Test of Adult Basic Education®

The TABE® exam is a computer based exam, composed of four sections, reading, computational mathematics, applied mathematics, and language.

Section	Time	Questions
Reading	25	25
Computational Math	15	25
Applied Math	25	25
Language	25	25

For complete details on the skills evaluated in each section, see the corresponding chapter below.

While we seek to make our guide as comprehensive as possible, it is important to note that like all entrance exams, the TABE® Exam might be adjusted at some future point. New material might be added, or content that is no longer relevant or applicable might be removed. It is always a good idea to give the materials you receive when you register to take the TABE® a careful review.

The TABE® Study Plan

Now that you have made the decision to take the TABE®, it is time to get started. Before you do another thing, you will need to figure out a plan of attack. The very best study tip is to start early! The longer the time period you devote to regular study practice, the more likely you will be to retain the material and be able to access it quickly. If you thought that 1x20 is the same as 2x10, guess what? It really is not, when it comes to study time. Reviewing material for just an hour per day over the course of 20 days is far better than studying for two hours a day for only 10 days. The more often you revisit a particular piece of information, the better you will know it. Not only will your grasp and understanding be better, but your ability to reach into your brain and quickly and efficiently pull out the tidbit you need, will be greatly enhanced as well.

The great Chinese scholar and philosopher Confucius believed that true knowledge could be defined as knowing both what you know and what you do not know. The first step in preparing for the TABE® Exam is to assess your strengths and weaknesses. You may already have an idea of what you know and what you do not know, but evaluating yourself using our Self- Assessment modules for each of the three areas, math, reading comprehension and essay writing, will clarify the details.

Making a Study Schedule
In order to make your study time most productive you will need to develop a study plan. The purpose of the plan is to organize all the bits of pieces of information in such a way that you will not feel overwhelmed. Rome was not built in a day, and learning everything you will need to know in order

to pass the TABE® Exam is going to take time, too. Arranging the material you need to learn into manageable chunks is the best way to go. Each study session should make you feel as though you have succeeded in accomplishing your goal, and your goal is simply to learn what you planned to learn during that particular session. Try to organize the content in such a way that each study session builds upon previous ones. That way, you will retain the information, be better able to access it, and review the previous bits and pieces at the same time.

Self-assessment

The Best Study Tip! The very best study tip is to start early! The longer you study regularly, the more you will retain and 'learn' the material. Studying for 1 hour per day for 20 days is far better than studying for 2 hours for 10 days.

What don't you know?

The first step is to assess your strengths and weaknesses. You may already have an idea of where your weaknesses are, or you can take our Self-assessment modules for each of the areas, math, reading comprehension and essay writing.

Exam Component	Rate from 1 to 5
Reading	
Main idea and supporting details	
Drawing inferences	
Mathematics	
Algebra	
Estimation	
Percent, Decimal, Fractions	
Word Problems	
Basic Geometry	
Word Problems	

Making a Study Schedule

The key to making a study plan is to divide the material you need to learn into manageable size and learn it, while at the same time reviewing the material that you already know.

Using the table above, any scores of three or below, you need to spend time learning, going over and practicing this subject area. A score of four means you need to review the material, but you don't have to spend time re-learning. A score of five and you are OK with just an occasional review before the exam.

A score of zero or one means you really do need to work on this and you should allocate the most time and give it the highest priority. Some students prefer a 5-day plan and others a 10-day plan. It also depends on how much time you have until the exam.

Here is an example of a 5-day plan based on an example from the table above:

Reading: 1   Study 1 hour everyday – review on last day
Fractions: 3   Study 1 hour for 2 days then ½ hour and then review
Algebra: 4   Review every second day
Word Problems (Applied Math) : 2 Study 1 hour on the first day – then ½ hour everyday
Basic Geometry: 5 Review for ½ hour every other day

Using this example, Basic Geometry is good and only needs occasional review. Algebra is good and needs 'some' review. Fractions need a bit of work, grammar and usage needs a lot of work and Reading is very weak and need the majority of time. Based on this, here is a sample study plan:

Day	Subject	Time
Monday		
Study	Reading	1 hour
Study	Word Problems	1 hour
	½ hour break	
Study	Fractions	1 hour
Review	Algebra	½ hour
Tuesday		
Study	Reading	1 hour
Study	Word Problems	½ hour
	½ hour break	
Study	Fractions	½ hour
Review	Algebra	½ hour
Review	Basic Geometry	½ hour
Wednesday		
Study	Reading	1 hour
Study	Word Problems	½ hour
	½ hour break	
Study	Fractions	½ hour
Review	Basic Geometry	½ hour
Thursday		
Study	Reading	½ hour
Study	Word Problems	½ hour
Review	Fractions	½ hour
	½ hour break	
Review	Basic Geometry	½ hour
Review	Algebra	½ hour
Friday		
Review	Reading	½ hour
Review	Word Problems	½ hour
Review	Fractions	½ hour
	½ hour break	
Review	Algebra	½ hour
Review	Word Problems	½ hour

Using this example, adapt the study plan to your own schedule. This schedule assumes 2 ½ - 3 hours available to study everyday for a 5 day period.

First, write out what you need to study and how much. Next figure out how many days you have before the test. Note, do NOT study on the last day before the test. On the last day before the test, you won't learn anything and will probably only confuse yourself.

Make a table with the days before the test and the number of hours you have available to study each day. We suggest working with 1 hour and ½ hour time slots.

Start filling in the blanks, with the subjects you need to study the most getting the most time and the most regular time slots (i.e. everyday) and the subjects that you know getting the least time (e.g. ½ hour every other day, or every 3rd day).

Tips for making a schedule

Once you make a schedule, stick with it! Make your study sessions reasonable. If you make a study schedule and don't stick with it, you set yourself up for failure. Instead, schedule study sessions that are a bit shorter and set yourself up for success! Make sure your study sessions are do-able. Studying is hard work but after you pass, you can party and take a break!

Schedule breaks. Breaks are just as important as study time. Work out a rotation of studying and breaks that works for you.

Build up study time. If you find it hard to sit still and study for 1 hour straight through, build up to it. Start with 20 minutes, and then take a break. Once you get used to 20-minute study sessions, increase the time to 30 minutes. Gradually work you way up to 1 hour.

40 minutes to 1 hour is optimal. Studying for longer than this is tiring and not productive. Studying for shorter isn't long enough to be productive.

Studying Math.   Studying Math is different from study-ing other subjects because you use a different part of your brain. The best way to study math is to practice everyday. This will train your mind to think in a mathematical way. If you miss a day or days, the mathematical mind-set is gone and you have to start all over again to build it up.

Study and practice math everyday for at least 5 days before the exam.

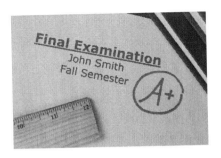

Practice Test Questions Set 1

The questions below are not exactly the same as you will find on the TABE® - that would be too easy! And nobody knows what the questions will be and they change all the time. Below are general questions that cover the same subject areas as the TABE®. So while the format and exact wording of the questions may differ slightly, and change from year to year, if you can answer the questions below, you will have no problem with the TABE®.

For the best results, take these Practice Test Questions as if it were the real exam. Set aside time when you will not be disturbed, and a location that is quiet and free of distractions. Read the instructions carefully, read each question carefully, and answer to the best of your ability.
Use the bubble answer sheets provided. When you have completed the Practice Questions, check your answer against the Answer Key and read the explanation provided.

Do not attempt more than one set of practice test questions in one day. After completing the first practice test, wait two or three days before attempting the second set of questions.

Reading

1. (A) (B) (C) (D)   11. (A) (B) (C) (D)   21. (A) (B) (C) (D)

2. (A) (B) (C) (D)   12. (A) (B) (C) (D)   22. (A) (B) (C) (D)

3. (A) (B) (C) (D)   13. (A) (B) (C) (D)   23. (A) (B) (C) (D)

4. (A) (B) (C) (D)   14. (A) (B) (C) (D)   24. (A) (B) (C) (D)

5. (A) (B) (C) (D)   15. (A) (B) (C) (D)   25. (A) (B) (C) (D)

6. (A) (B) (C) (D)   16. (A) (B) (C) (D)

7. (A) (B) (C) (D)   17. (A) (B) (C) (D)

8. (A) (B) (C) (D)   18. (A) (B) (C) (D)

9. (A) (B) (C) (D)   19. (A) (B) (C) (D)

10. (A) (B) (C) (D)   20. (A) (B) (C) (D)

Computational Mathematics

1. Ⓐ Ⓑ Ⓒ Ⓓ   11. Ⓐ Ⓑ Ⓒ Ⓓ   21. Ⓐ Ⓑ Ⓒ Ⓓ

2. Ⓐ Ⓑ Ⓒ Ⓓ   12. Ⓐ Ⓑ Ⓒ Ⓓ   22. Ⓐ Ⓑ Ⓒ Ⓓ

3. Ⓐ Ⓑ Ⓒ Ⓓ   13. Ⓐ Ⓑ Ⓒ Ⓓ   23. Ⓐ Ⓑ Ⓒ Ⓓ

4. Ⓐ Ⓑ Ⓒ Ⓓ   14. Ⓐ Ⓑ Ⓒ Ⓓ   24. Ⓐ Ⓑ Ⓒ Ⓓ

5. Ⓐ Ⓑ Ⓒ Ⓓ   15. Ⓐ Ⓑ Ⓒ Ⓓ   25. Ⓐ Ⓑ Ⓒ Ⓓ

6. Ⓐ Ⓑ Ⓒ Ⓓ   16. Ⓐ Ⓑ Ⓒ Ⓓ

7. Ⓐ Ⓑ Ⓒ Ⓓ   17. Ⓐ Ⓑ Ⓒ Ⓓ

8. Ⓐ Ⓑ Ⓒ Ⓓ   18. Ⓐ Ⓑ Ⓒ Ⓓ

9. Ⓐ Ⓑ Ⓒ Ⓓ   19. Ⓐ Ⓑ Ⓒ Ⓓ

10. Ⓐ Ⓑ Ⓒ Ⓓ   20. Ⓐ Ⓑ Ⓒ Ⓓ

Applied Mathematics

1. (A) (B) (C) (D)   11. (A) (B) (C) (D)   21. (A) (B) (C) (D)

2. (A) (B) (C) (D)   12. (A) (B) (C) (D)   22. (A) (B) (C) (D)

3. (A) (B) (C) (D)   13. (A) (B) (C) (D)   23. (A) (B) (C) (D)

4. (A) (B) (C) (D)   14. (A) (B) (C) (D)   24. (A) (B) (C) (D)

5. (A) (B) (C) (D)   15. (A) (B) (C) (D)   25. (A) (B) (C) (D)

6. (A) (B) (C) (D)   16. (A) (B) (C) (D)

7. (A) (B) (C) (D)   17. (A) (B) (C) (D)

8. (A) (B) (C) (D)   18. (A) (B) (C) (D)

9. (A) (B) (C) (D)   19. (A) (B) (C) (D)

10. (A) (B) (C) (D)   20. (A) (B) (C) (D)

Language

1. Ⓐ Ⓑ Ⓒ Ⓓ 11. Ⓐ Ⓑ Ⓒ Ⓓ 21. Ⓐ Ⓑ Ⓒ Ⓓ 31. Ⓐ Ⓑ Ⓒ Ⓓ

2. Ⓐ Ⓑ Ⓒ Ⓓ 12. Ⓐ Ⓑ Ⓒ Ⓓ 22. Ⓐ Ⓑ Ⓒ Ⓓ 32. Ⓐ Ⓑ Ⓒ Ⓓ

3. Ⓐ Ⓑ Ⓒ Ⓓ 13. Ⓐ Ⓑ Ⓒ Ⓓ 23. Ⓐ Ⓑ Ⓒ Ⓓ 33. Ⓐ Ⓑ Ⓒ Ⓓ

4. Ⓐ Ⓑ Ⓒ Ⓓ 14. Ⓐ Ⓑ Ⓒ Ⓓ 24. Ⓐ Ⓑ Ⓒ Ⓓ 34. Ⓐ Ⓑ Ⓒ Ⓓ

5. Ⓐ Ⓑ Ⓒ Ⓓ 15. Ⓐ Ⓑ Ⓒ Ⓓ 25. Ⓐ Ⓑ Ⓒ Ⓓ 35. Ⓐ Ⓑ Ⓒ Ⓓ

6. Ⓐ Ⓑ Ⓒ Ⓓ 16. Ⓐ Ⓑ Ⓒ Ⓓ 26. Ⓐ Ⓑ Ⓒ Ⓓ 36. Ⓐ Ⓑ Ⓒ Ⓓ

7. Ⓐ Ⓑ Ⓒ Ⓓ 17. Ⓐ Ⓑ Ⓒ Ⓓ 27. Ⓐ Ⓑ Ⓒ Ⓓ 37. Ⓐ Ⓑ Ⓒ Ⓓ

8. Ⓐ Ⓑ Ⓒ Ⓓ 18. Ⓐ Ⓑ Ⓒ Ⓓ 28. Ⓐ Ⓑ Ⓒ Ⓓ 38. Ⓐ Ⓑ Ⓒ Ⓓ

9. Ⓐ Ⓑ Ⓒ Ⓓ 19. Ⓐ Ⓑ Ⓒ Ⓓ 29. Ⓐ Ⓑ Ⓒ Ⓓ 39. Ⓐ Ⓑ Ⓒ Ⓓ

10. Ⓐ Ⓑ Ⓒ Ⓓ 20. Ⓐ Ⓑ Ⓒ Ⓓ 30. Ⓐ Ⓑ Ⓒ Ⓓ 40. Ⓐ Ⓑ Ⓒ Ⓓ

Reading and Language Arts

Questions 1 – 4 refer to the following passage.

Infectious Diseases

An infectious disease is a clinically evident illness resulting from the presence of pathogenic agents, such as viruses, bacteria, fungi, protozoa, multi-cellular parasites, and unusual proteins known as prions. Infectious pathologies are also called communicable diseases or transmissible diseases, due to their potential of transmission from one person or species to another by a replicating agent (as opposed to a toxin).

Transmission of an infectious disease can occur in many different ways. Physical contact, liquids, food, body fluids, contaminated objects, and airborne inhalation can all transmit infecting agents.

Transmissible diseases that occur through contact with an ill person, or objects touched by them, are especially infective, and are sometimes referred to as contagious diseases. Communicable diseases that require a more specialized route of infection, such as through blood or needle transmission, or sexual transmission, are usually not regarded as contagious.

The term infectivity describes the ability of an organism to enter, survive and multiply in the host, while the infectiousness of a disease indicates the comparative ease with which the disease is transmitted. An infection however, is not synonymous with an infectious disease, as an infection may not cause important clinical symptoms. [3]

1. What can we infer from the first paragraph in this passage?

    a. Sickness from a toxin can be easily transmitted from one person to another.

    b. Sickness from an infectious disease can be easily transmitted from one person to another.

    c. Few sicknesses are transmitted from one person to another.

    d. Infectious diseases are easily treated.

2. What are two other names for infections' pathologies?

    a. Communicable diseases or transmissible diseases

    b. Communicable diseases or terminal diseases

    c. Transmissible diseases or preventable diseases

    d. Communicative diseases or unstable diseases

3. What does infectivity describe?

    a. The inability of an organism to multiply in the host

    b. The inability of an organism to reproduce

    c. The ability of an organism to enter, survive and multiply in the host

    d. The ability of an organism to reproduce in the host

4. How do we know an infection is not synonymous with an infectious disease?

    a. Because an infectious disease destroys infections with enough time.

    b. Because an infection may not cause clinical symptoms or impair host function.

    c. We do not. The two are synonymous.

    d. Because an infection is too fatal to be an infectious disease.

Questions 5 – 7 refer to the following passage.

The US Weather Service

The United States National Weather Service classifies thunderstorms as severe when they reach a predetermined level. Usually, this means the storm is strong enough to inflict wind or hail damage. In most of the United States, a storm is considered severe if winds reach over 50 knots (58 mph or 93 km/h), hail is ¾ inch (2 cm) diameter or larger, or if meteorologists report funnel clouds or tornadoes. In the Central Region of the United States National Weather Service, the hail threshold for a severe thunderstorm is 1 inch (2.5 cm) in diameter. Though a funnel cloud or tornado indicates the presence of a severe thunderstorm, the various meteorological agencies would issue a tornado warning rather than a severe thunderstorm warning in this case.

Meteorologists in Canada define a severe thunderstorm as either having tornadoes, wind gusts of 90 km/h or greater, hail 2 centimeters in diameter or greater, rainfall more than 50 millimeters in 1 hour, or 75 millimeters in 3 hours.

Severe thunderstorms can develop from any type of thunderstorm. [4]

5. What is the purpose of this passage?

a. Explaining when a thunderstorm turns into a tornado

b. Explaining who issues storm warnings, and when these warnings should be issued

c. Explaining when meteorologists consider a thunderstorm severe

d. None of the above

6. It is possible to infer from this passage that

a. Different areas and countries have different criteria for determining a severe storm

b. Thunderstorms can include lightning and tornadoes, as well as violent winds and large hail

c. If someone spots both a thunderstorm and a tornado, meteorological agencies will immediately issue a severe storm warning

d. Canada has a much different alert system for severe storms, with criteria that are far less

7. What would the Central Region of the United States National Weather Service do if hail was 2.7 cm in diameter?

a. Not issue a severe thunderstorm warning.

b. Issue a tornado warning.

c. Issue a severe thunderstorm warning.

d. Sleet must also accompany the hail before the Weather Service will issue a storm warning.

Question 8 refers to the following passage.

Contents

8. Consider the table of contents above. What page would you find information about natural selection and adaptation?

    a. 81

    b. 90

    c. 110

    d. 132

Questions 9 – 11 refer to the following passage.

Clouds

A cloud is a visible mass of droplets or frozen crystals floating in the atmosphere above the surface of the Earth or other planetary bodies. Another type of cloud is a mass of material in space, attracted by gravity, called interstellar clouds and nebulae. The branch of meteorology which studies clouds is called nephrology. When we are speaking of Earth clouds, water vapor is usually the condensing substance, which forms small droplets or ice crystal. These crystals are typically 0.01 mm in diameter. Dense, deep clouds reflect most light, so they appear white, at least from the top. Cloud droplets scatter light very efficiently, so the further into a cloud light travels, the weaker it gets. This accounts for the gray or dark appearance at the base of large clouds. Thin clouds may appear to have acquired the color of their environment or background. [5]

9. What are clouds made of?

    a. Water droplets.

    b. Ice crystals.

    c. Ice crystals and water droplets.

    d. Clouds on Earth are made of ice crystals and water droplets.

10. The main idea of this passage is

a. Condensation occurs in clouds, having an intense effect on the weather on the surface of the earth.

b. Atmospheric gases are responsible for the gray color of clouds just before a severe storm happens.

c. A cloud is a visible mass of droplets or frozen crystals floating in the atmosphere above the surface of the Earth or other planetary body.

d. Clouds reflect light in varying amounts and degrees, depending on the size and concentration of the water droplets.

11. Why are clouds white on top and grey on the bottom?

a. Because water droplets inside the cloud do not reflect light, it appears white, and the further into the cloud the light travels, the less light is reflected making the bottom appear dark.

b. Because water droplets outside the cloud reflect light, it appears dark, and the further into the cloud the light travels, the more light is reflected making the bottom appear white.

c. Because water droplets inside the cloud reflects light, making it appear white, and the further into the cloud the light travels, the more light is reflected making the bottom appear dark.

d. None of the above.

Questions 12 - 15 refer to the following recipe.

The Civil War

The Civil War began on April 12, 1861. The first shots of the Civil War were fired in Fort Sumter, South Carolina. It is interesting to note that even though more American lives were lost in the Civil War than in any other war, not one person died on that first day. The war began because eleven Southern states seceded from the Union and tried to start their own government, The Confederate States of America.

Why did the states secede? The issue of slavery was a primary cause of the Civil War. The eleven southern states relied heavily on their slaves in order to foster their farming and plantation lifestyles. The northern states, many of whom had already abolished slavery, did not feel that the southern states should have slaves. The north wanted to free all the slaves and President Lincoln's goal was to both end slavery and preserve the Union. He had Congress declare war on the Confederacy on April 14, 1862. For four long, blood soaked years, the North and South fought against each other.

From 1861 to mid 1863, it seemed as if the South would win this war. However, on July 1, 1863, an epic three day battle was waged on a field in Gettysburg, Pennsylvania. Gettysburg is remembered for being one of the bloodiest battles in American history. At the end of the three days, the North turned the tide of the war in their favor. The North then went on to dominate the South for the remainder of the war. Most well remembered might be General Sherman's "March to The Sea", where he famously led the Union Army through Georgia and the Carolinas, burning and destroying everything in their path.

In 1865, the Union army invaded and captured the Confederate capital of Richmond Virginia. Robert E. Lee, leader of the Confederacy surrendered to General Ulysses S. Grant, leader of the Union forces, on April 9, 1865. The Civil War was over and the Union was preserved.

12. What does secede mean?

    a. To break away from

    b. To accomplish

    c. To join

    d. To lose

13. Which of the following statements summarizes a FACT from the passage?

    a. Congress declared war and then the Battle of Fort Sumter began.

    b. Congress declared war after shots were fired at Fort Sumter.

    c. President Lincoln was pro slavery

    d. President Lincoln was at Fort Sumter with Congress

14. Which event finally led the Confederacy to surrender?

    a. The battle of Gettysburg

    b. The battle of Bull Run

    c. The invasion of the confederate capital of Richmond

    d. Sherman's March to the Sea

15. The word abolish as used in this passage most nearly means?

    a. To ban

    b. To polish

    c. To support

    d. To destroy

Questions 16 – 20 refer to the following passage.

Navy Seals

The United States Navy's Sea, Air and Land Teams, commonly known as Navy SEALs, are the U.S. Navy's principal special operations force, and a part of the Naval Special Warfare Command (NSWC) as well as the maritime component of the United States Special Operations Command (USSOCOM).

The unit's acronym ("SEAL") comes from their capacity to operate at sea, in the air, and on land – but it is their ability to work underwater that separates SEALs from most other military units in the world. Navy SEALs are trained and have been deployed in a wide variety of missions, including direct action and special reconnaissance operations, unconventional warfare, foreign internal defence, hostage rescue, counter-terrorism and other missions. All SEALs are members of either the United States Navy or the United States Coast Guard.

In the early morning of May 2, 2011 local time, a team of 40 CIA-led Navy SEALs completed an operation to kill Osama bin Laden in Abbottabad, Pakistan about 35 miles (56 km) from Islamabad, the country's capital. The Navy SEALs were part of the Naval Special Warfare Development Group, previously called "Team 6". President Barack Obama later confirmed the death of bin Laden. The unprecedented media coverage raised the public profile of the SEAL community, particularly the counter-terrorism specialists commonly known as SEAL Team 6. [6]

16. Are Navy SEALs part of USSOCOM?

    a. Yes

    b. No

    c. Only for special operations

    d. No, they are part of the US Navy

17. What separates Navy SEALs from other military units?

    a. Belonging to NSWC

    b. Direct action and special reconnaissance operations

    c. Working underwater

    d. Working for other military units in the world

18. What other military organizations do SEALs belong to?

    a. The US Navy

    b. The Coast Guard

    c. The US Army

    d. The Navy and the Coast Guard

19. What other organization participated in the Bin Laden raid?

    a. The CIA

    b. The US Military

    c. Counter-terrorism specialists

    d. None of the above

20. What is the new name for Team 6?

    a. They were always called Team 6

    b. The counter-terrorism specialists

    c. The Naval Special Warfare Development Group

    d. None of the above

Questions 21 – 23 refer to the following passage.

How To Get A Good Nights Sleep

Sleep is just as essential for healthy living as water, air and food. Sleep allows the body to rest and replenish depleted energy levels. Sometimes we may for various reasons experience difficulty sleeping which has a serious effect on our health. Those who have prolonged sleeping problems are facing a serious medical condition and should see a qualified doctor as soon as possible for help. Here is simple guide that can help you sleep better at night.

Try to create a natural pattern of waking up and sleeping

around the same time everyday. This means avoiding going to bed too early and oversleeping past your usual wake
up time. Going to bed and getting up at radically different
times everyday confuses your body clock. Try to establish a
natural rhythm as much as you can.

Exercises and a bit of physical activity can help you sleep
better at night. If you are having problem sleeping, try to be
as active as you can during the day. If you are tired from
physical activity, falling asleep is a natural and easy process
for your body. If you remain inactive during the day, you
will find it harder to sleep properly at night. Try walking, jog-
ging, swimming or simple stretches as you get close to your
bed time.

Afternoon naps are great to refresh you during the day, but
they may also keep you awake at night. If you feel sleepy
during the day, get up, take a walk and get busy to keep
from sleeping. Stretching is a good way to increase blood
flow to the brain and keep you alert so that you don't sleep
during the day. This will help you sleep better night.

> A warm bath or a glass of milk in the evening
> can help your body relax and prepare for
> sleep. A cold bath will wake you up and keep
> you up for several hours. Also avoid eating too
> late before bed.

21. How would you describe this sentence?

  a. A recommendation

  b. An opinion

  c. A fact

  d. A diagnosis

22. Which of the following is an alternative title for this article?

    a. Exercise and a good night's sleep

    b. Benefits of a good night's sleep

    c. Tips for a good night's sleep

    d. Lack of sleep is a serious medical condition

23. Which of the following can not be inferred from this article?

    a. Biking is helpful for getting a good night's sleep

    b. Mental activity is helpful for getting a good night's sleep

    c. Eating bedtime snacks is not recommended

    d. Getting up at the same time is helpful for a good night's sleep

Questions 24 – 25 refer to the following graphic.

Save the Children

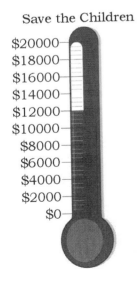

24. Consider the graphic above. The Save the Children fund has a fund-raising goal of $20,000. Approximately how much of their goal have they achieved?

    a. 3/5

    b. 3/4

    c. 1/2

    d. 1/3

25. Consider the graphic above. The Save the Children fund has a fund-raising goal of $16,000. Approximately how much of their goal have they achieved?

    a. 3/5

    b. 3/4

    c. 1/2

    d. 1/3

Computational Mathematics

1. What fraction of $1500 is $75?

    a. 1/14

    b. 3/5

    c. 7/10

    d. 1/20

2. Estimate 215 x 65.

    a. 1,350

    b. 13,500

    c. 103,500

    d. 3,500

3. Below is the attendance for a class of 45.

Day	Number of Absent Students
Monday	5
Tuesday	9
Wednesday	4
Thursday	10
Friday	6

What is the average attendance for the week?

     a. 88%

     b. 85%

     c. 81%

     d. 77%

4. 2/3 – 2/5 =

     a. 4/10

     b. 1/15

     c. 3/7

     d. 4/15

5. Express 0.27 + 0.33 as a fraction.

     a. 3/6

     b. 4/7

     c. 3/5

     d. 2/7

6. $7^5 - 3^5 =$

    a. 15,000

    b. 16,564

    c. 15,800

    d. 15,007

7. What is 2/4 X 3/4 reduced to lowest terms?

    a. 6/12

    b. 3/8

    c. 6/16

    d. 3/4

8. Solve the following equation 4(y + 6) = 3y + 30

    a. y = 20

    b. y = 6

    c. y = 30/7

    d. y = 30

9. 2/3 of 60 + 1/5 of 75 =

    a. 45

    b. 55

    c. 15

    d. 50

10. What is 1/3 of 3/4?

    a. 1/4

    b. 1/3

    c. 2/3

    d. 3/4

11. **What is (3.13 + 7.87) X 5?**

    a. 65

    b. 50

    c. 45

    d. 55

12. **Express 5 x 5 x 5 x 5 x 5 x 5 in exponential form.**

    a. 5^6

    b. 10^6

    c. 5^{16}

    d. 5^3

13. **Express 9 x 9 x 9 in exponential form and standard form.**

    a. $9^3 = 719$

    b. $9^3 = 629$

    c. $9^3 = 729$

    d. $10^3 = 729$

14. **If y = 4 and x = 3, solve yx^3**

    a. -108

    b. 108

    c. 27

    d. 4

15. **Divide 0.524 by 10^3**

    a. 0.0524

    b. 0.000524

    c. 0.00524

    d. 524

16. Solve 3x – 27 = 0

    a. x = 24

    b. x = 30

    c. x = 9

    d. x = 21

17. Which of the following is between 7/11 and 5/7?

    a. 0.6

    b. 13/17

    c. 2/3

    d. 11/15

18. Solve: 0.25 + 0.65

    a. 1/2

    b. 9/10

    c. 4/7

    d. 2/9

19. 389 + 454 =

    a. 853

    b. 833

    c. 843

    d. 863

20. 9,177 + 7,204 =

    a. 16,4712

    b. 16,371

    c. 16,381

    d. 15,412

21. 2,199 + 5,832 =

    a. 8,331

    b. 8,041

    c. 8,141

    d. 8,031

22. 8,390 - 5,239 =

    a. 3,261

    b. 3,151

    c. 3,161

    d. 3,101

23. 643 - 587 =

    a. 56

    b. 66

    c. 46

    d. 55

24. 3,406 - 2,767 =

    a. 629

    b. 720

    c. 639

    d. 649

25. 149 × 7 =

    a. 1032

    b. 1043

    c. 1059

    d. 1063

Applied Mathematics

1. A square box measures 20 cm long and 20 cm wide and 20 cm high. What is the volume of the box?

    a. 60 cm³

    b. 20,000 cm³

    c. 4,000 cm³

    d. 8,000 cm³

2. A worker's weekly salary was increased by 30%. If his new salary is $150, what was his old salary?

    a. $120.00

    b. $99.15

    c. $109.00

    d. $115.40

3. Mr. Jones runs a factory. His total assets are $256,800 which consists of a building worth $80,500, machinery worth $125.000 and $51,300 cash. After one year what will be the value of his total assets if he has additional cash of $75,600 and the value of his building has increased by 10% per year, and his machinery depreciated by 20%?

    a. $243,450

    b. $252,450

    c. $264,150

    d. $272,350

4. Brad has agreed to buy everyone a Coke. Each drink costs $1.89, and there are 5 friends. Estimate Brad's cost.

    a. $7

    b. $8

    c. $10

    d. $12

5. The manager of a weaving factory estimates that if 10 machines run at 100% efficiency for 8 hours, they will produce 1450 meters of cloth. Due to some technical problems, 4 machines run of 95% efficiency and the remaining 6 at 90% efficiency. How many meters of cloth can these machines will produce in 8 hours?

    a. 1479 meters

    b. 1310 meters

    c. 1300 meters

    d. 1285 meters

6. My current pay is 'x' dollars. Every month it is increased 0.5%. After 'y' months, what will my pay be?

    a. X + 0.005xy

    b. 1.002xy

    c. X + 1.005xy/y

    d. X + 1.005xy/y

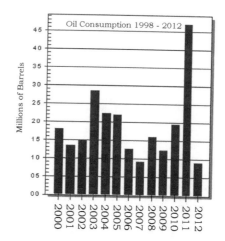

7. The graph above shows oil consumption in millions of barrels for the period, 1998 - 2012. What year did oil consumption peak?

    a. 2011

    b. 2010

    c. 2008

    d. 2009

8. In a local election at polling station A, 945 voters cast their vote out of 1270 registered voters. At polling station B, 860 cast their vote out of 1050 registered voters and at station C, 1210 cast their vote out of 1440 registered voters. What is the total turnout from all three polling stations?

    a. 70%

    b. 74%

    c. 76%

    d. 80%

9. A pet store sold $19,304.56 worth of merchandise in June. If the cost of products sold was $5,284.34, employees were paid $8,384.76, and rent was $2,920.00, how much profit did the store make in June?

    a. $5,635.46

    b. $2,714.46

    c. $14,020.22

    d. $10,019.80

    e) $16,383.57

10. A small lot has a perimeter of 100 feet. What's the area, expressed in square feet?

    a. We cannot tell from this information.

    b. 10 ft^2

    c. 400 ft^2

    d. 100 ft^2

11. John is a barber and receives 40% of the amount paid by each of his customers. John gets all of any tips paid to him. If a man pays $8.50 for a haircut and pays a tip of $1.30, how much money goes to John?

    a. $3.92

    b. $4.70

    c. $5.30

    d. $6.40

12. Mr. Jones bought 5 children's tickets and 9 adult tickets to the zoo. He paid a total of $67. Mr. Jackson paid $38.50 for 7 adult tickets. What is the cost of each type of ticket?

a. adult = $13.40 and children = $47.44

b. adult = $7.44 and children = $13.40

c. adult = $3.50 and children = $5.50

d. adult = $5.50 and children = $3.50

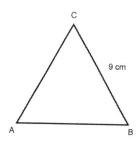

13. What is the perimeter of the equilateral △ABC above?

a. 18 cm

b. 12 cm

c. 27 cm

d. 15 cm

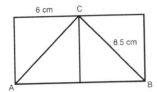

14. What is perimeter of ΔABC in the above shape?

    a. 25.5 cm

    b. 27 cm

    c. 30 cm

    d. 29 cm

15. A woman spent 15% of her income on an item and ends up with $120. What percentage of her income is left?

    a. 12%

    b. 85%

    c. 75%

    d. 95%

16. A rectangular box measures at 10 cm long and 8 cm wide and 10 cm high. What is the volume of the box?

    a. 28 cm^3

    b. 2000 cm^3

    c. 400 cm^3

    d. 800 cm^3

17. At the beginning of 2009, Marilyn invested $5,000 in a savings account. The account pays 4% interest per year. At the end 2 years, how much did Marilyn have in the account?

    a. $5,200

    b. $5,408

    c. $5,110

    d. $7,000

18. A distributor purchased 550 kilogram potatoes of $165. He distributed all these at a rate of $6.4 per 20 kilograms to 15 shops, $3.4 per 10 kilograms to 12 shops and remaining at $1.8. If his distribution cast is $10 then what will be his profit?

    a. $10.4

    b. $13.6

    c. $14.9

    d. $23.4

19. A car covers a distance in 3.5 hours with average speed of 60 km/hr. How much time in hours a motorbike will take to cover this distance with average speed of 40km/hr?

    a. 6 hours

    b. 5 hours

    c. 5.5 hours

    d. 5.25 hours

20. Write 51.738 to the nearest 100th.

    a. 51.735

    b. 51.7

    c. 51.73

    d. 51.74

21. What is the ratio between 2 gold coins, 6 silver coins and 12 bronze coins?

    a. 2:3:4

    b. 1:2:4

    c. 1:3:4

    d. 2:3:4

22. Choose the expression the figure represents.

    a. X < 1

    b. X < 1

    c. X > 1

    d. X > 1

23. Choose the expression the figure represents.

    a. X > 2

    b. X > 2

    c. X < 2

    d. X < 2

24. Convert 7,892,000,000 to scientific notation.

    a. 7.892×10^{10}

    b. 7.892×10^{-9}

    c. 7.892×10^{9}

    d. 0.7892×10^{11}

25. Consider the following sequence:

+ * + * | * + * + | * * + * | + + __ __

    a. + *

    b. * *

    c. + +

    d. * +

English

For questions 1 - 5, fill in the blank with the correct punctuation.

1. Watch out for the broken glass _____

    a. .

    b. ?

    c. ,

    d. !

2. We saw many beautiful sights on our vacation_____ but we spent too many hours on the road.

    a. ,

    b. :

    c. ;

    d. .

3. She loved fresh vegetables at dinner _____ he wanted only meat on his dinner table.

    a. ,

    b. :

    c. ;

    d. .

4. Cautiously, he investigated the noise _____ but it was only the cat scratching the door.

    a. !

    b. :

    c. ;

    d. .

5. We packed a tent, several sleeping bags, a stove _____ and plenty of foods.

    a. ,

    b. :

    c. ;

    d. .

6. Choose the sentence below with the correct punctuation.

    a. George wrecked John's car that was the end of their friendship.

    b. George wrecked John's car. that was the end of their friendship.

    c. George wrecked John's car; that was the end of their friendship.

    d. None of the above

7. Choose the sentence below with the correct punctuation.

a. The dress was not Gina's favorite; however, she wore it to the dance.

b. The dress was not Gina's favorite, however, she wore it to the dance.

c. The dress was not Gina's favorite, however; she wore it to the dance.

d. The dress was not Gina's favorite however, she wore it to the dance.

8. Choose the sentence below with the correct punctuation.

a. Chris showed his dedication to golf in many ways, for example, he watched all of the tournaments on television.

b. Chris showed his dedication to golf in many ways; for example, he watched all of the   tournaments on television.

c. Chris showed his dedication to golf in many ways, for example; he watched all of the tournaments on television.

d. Chris showed his dedication to golf in many ways for example he watched all of the tournaments on television.

9. Choose the sentence below with the correct punctuation.

   a. There are many species of owls, the Great-Horned Owl, the Snowy Owl, and the Western Screech Owl, and the Barn Owl.

   b. There are many species of owls, the Great-Horned Owl: the Snowy Owl: and the Western Screech Owl, and the Barn Owl.

   c. There are many species of owls; the Great-Horned Owl, the Snowy Owl, and the Western Screech Owl, and the Barn Owl.

   d. There are many species of owls: the Great-Horned Owl, the Snowy Owl, the Western Screech Owl, and the Barn Owl.

10. Choose the sentence below with the correct punctuation.

   a. In his most famous speech, Reverend King proclaimed: "I have a dream!"

   b. In his most famous speech, Reverend King proclaimed; "I have a dream!"

   c. In his most famous speech, Reverend King proclaimed. "I have a dream!"

   d. In his most famous speech: Reverend King proclaimed, "I have a dream!"

11. Choose the sentence with the correct punctuation and capitalization.

   a. "How often do you read the newspaper?" his father asked.

   b. How often do you read the newspaper. His father asked.

   c. "How often do you read the newspaper, his father asked?

   d. How often do you read the newspaper his father asked.

12. Choose the sentence with the correct punctuation and capitalization.

a. The City of Miami is not the capital of Florida.

b. Tallahassee has been the capital of florida since 1,824.

c. Where can I find Californias best beaches?

d. My parents used to live in brooklyn, New York.

13. Choose the sentence with the correct punctuation and capitalization.

a. The Wall street journal and New York times are popular newspapers.

b. I read the Chicago Tribune every day.

c. Mr Smith has the Weekend Newspaper delivered to his home.

d. Usa Today is published by the Gannett Company.

14. Choose the sentence with the correct punctuation and capitalization.

a. The ANB is the bank, the only bank, that I trust with my money.

b. The ANB is the bank; The Only Bank; that I trust with my money.

c. The ANB is the bank the only bank that I trust with my money.

d. The ANB is the bank – the only bank that I trust with my money.

15. Choose the sentence with the correct punctuation and capitalization.

    a. John Legend performed "All of Me" at the 2014 Grammys.

    b. John Legend performed All of Me at the Grammys.

    c. John Legend performed – All of Me – at the Grammys.

    d. John Legend Performed "All of me at the 2014 Grammys."

16. Combine the following two sentences into one sentence with the same meaning.

He writes poetry.
He plays sports.

    a. He writes poetry as well as sports.

    b. He writes poetry instead of playing sports.

    c. He not only writes poetry, but also plays sports.

    d. He writes poetry in order to play sports.

17. Combine the following two sentences into one sentence with the same meaning.

The student was punished.
The student was rude to the teacher.

    a. The student was punished as a result of being rude to the teacher.

    b. Even if the student was rude to the teacher, he was punished.

    c. Because the student was punished, he was rude to the teacher.

    d. The student was rude to the teacher but he was punished.

18. Combine the following two sentences into one sentence with the same meaning.

He failed his exam
He is quite lazy.

    a. He is quite lazy after he failed his exam.

    b. He failed his exam because he is quite lazy.

    c. Although he failed his exam he is quite lazy.

    d. Only if he failed his exam he is quite lazy.

19. Combine the following two sentences into one sentence with the same meaning.

Paolo will not be allowed to go.
Paolo has not completed his chores.

    a. Despite Paolo not completing his chores, he will not be allowed to go.

    b. Paolo has not completed his chores, although he will not be allowed to go.

    c. So that Paolo has not completed his chores, he will not be allowed to go.

    d. If Paolo has not completed his chores, he will not be allowed to go.

20. Combine the following two sentences into one sentence with the same meaning.

My mother picked up her car keys.
My mother plans to drive to the store.

a. My mother picked up her car keys as she plans to drive to the store.

b. When my mother plans to drive to the store she pick up her car keys.

c. Even if my mother picked up her car keys, she plans to drive to the store.

d. My mother picked up her car keys but she plans to drive to the store.

Directions: For questions 21 - 24 below, you are given a topic sentence. Choose the sentence which best develops the given topic sentence.

21. Acquiring real estate is an important investment.

a. Interest rates on mortgage are at an all-time low.

b. Older homes have a certain aesthetic appeal to mature buyers.

c. This decision should be made only after thorough research.

d. Banks usual don't give mortgages to unqualified individuals.

22. Taking vacations together helps to strengthen family bonds.

    a. Many families choose to book their flights months in advance.

    b. Travelling by plane is can be expensive and unsafe.

    c. Members return home with a fresh perspective on life.

    d. Children enjoy vacations because it's a time to have fun.

23. Global economic imbalances have contributed to poverty.

    a. 75 percent of America's wealth is controlled by the richest ten percent.

    b. Clean drinking water is scarce in some developing countries.

    c. Many people in the poorest countries die from hunger daily.

    d. Unemployment and illiteracy are on the rise globally.

24. A job interview is a potential employee's chance to make a good impression.

    a. Managers sometimes fire employees because of misconduct.

    b. A first degree is no longer enough to qualify for certain jobs.

    c. Employers usually prefer interviewees with experience.

    d. Interviewees are first judged by how they are dressed.

25. Player performance and behavior affect attendance at NBA matches.

    a. Michael Jordan is the best basketball player of all time.

    b. Disenchanted fans often stay away as a form of protest.

    c. Though games are televised, the court side experience is better.

    d. The NBA lays out strict rules that players must follow on court.

Questions 26 - 30 refer to the following passage.

Read the passage below and look at the numbered, underlined phrases. Choose the answer that is written correctly for each underlined part.

Insects, like humans, assimilate themselves into communities. Humans, as well as insects (26), divide labor among the individual members, with individuals or members carrying out unique roles, responsibilities or functions. Not all humans are equipt by (27) the same skills. Neither are all insects within the same community or colony. In some colonies the function of some insects are for reproduction (28), others carry out the day to day labor such as collecting food or constructing homes, and still others function as protectors or defenders, ensuring the overall safety of the community. Humans too have their assigned functions within their communities. There are construction workers which provide homes for the rest of the community to dwell in. There are farmers who produce the food to feed the community. There are police, soldiers and security guards that see about the safety of the community. Of course, in human communities, unlike among insects, there is significant overlap in functions. The human who gathers food in the field also builds the home and keeps it safe. However neither male humans nor most male insects, no matter how much they may desire it, are able to take on the reproductive role.

One difference over insect and human communities (29) is

the principle of working together for the communal good. Among insect colonies, such as termites and ants, all efforts are united to achieve the community goal. Humans generally don't work together for the common goal, except it involves a job for which they are being paid.

Insects are innately programed to carry out their duties. From observations there is never a sense of being cheated or wanting to advance ahead of the colony into a role of superiority. Television shows may depict human character traits in insects but that's all a farce. Insects do not have the ability to develop those patterns of behavior. Perhaps its high time (30) humans really learn from insects.

26. Choose the correct version.

    a. Humans, moreover insects

    b. Humans, also as insects

    c. Humans, additional insects

    d. Correct as is.

27. Choose the correct version.

    a. humans are equipped with

    b. humans are equipped by

    c. humans are equipt with

    d. Correct as is.

28. Choose the correct version.

    a. the function of some insects were for reproduction

    b. the functions of some insects is for reproduction

    c. the function of some insect is for reproductions

    d. Correct as is.

29. Choose the correct version.

a. difference among insect and human communities

b. difference from insect and human communities

c. difference between insect and human communities

d. Correct as is.

30. Choose the correct version.

a. Perhaps it's high time

b. Perhaps it'll be high time

c. Perhaps its' high time

d. Correct as is.

31. When Craig's dog was struck by a car, he rushed his pet to the _____.

a. Emergency room

b. Doctor

c. Veterinarian

d. Podiatrist

32. After she received her influenza vaccination, Nan thought that she was _____ to the common cold.

a. Immune

b. Susceptible

c. Vulnerable

d. At risk

33. Paul's rose bushes were being destroyed by Japanese beetles, so he invested in a good _____.

    a. Fungicide

    b. Fertilizer

    c. Sprinkler

    d. Pesticide

34. The last time that the crops failed, the entire nation experienced months of _____.

    a. Famine

    b. Harvest

    c. Plentitude

    d. Disease

35. Because of a pituitary dysfunction, Karl lacked the necessary _____ to grow as tall as his father.

    a. Glands

    b. Hormones

    c. Vitamins

    d. Testosterone

For questions 36 - 40, choose the word that best completes both sentences.

36. He never agrees with his political party. He has a reputation as a _____.

Her reputation as a _____ often gets her into trouble.

    a. Maverick

    b. Conformist

    c. Insider

    d. None of the above

37. With 8 kids, their house is always _____.

The 50% off sale was _____.

  a. Noisy
  b. Orderly
  c. Pandemonium
  d. None of the above

38. The water slowly _____ into the earth.

Don't worry it will _____ in a few minutes.

  a. Degenerate
  b. Dissipate
  c. Scatter
  d. None of the above

39. His skinny frame and _____ face scared me.

His eyes were sunken and his face was _____ .

  a. Gaunt
  b. Straight
  c. Sallow
  d. None of the above

40. The _____ was much more than I expected.

Your _____ will be paid at the end of the day.

  a. Donation
  b. Remuneration
  c. Warning
  d. None of the above

41. High performance cars like that require constant _____.

    a. Maintainance

    b. Maintenace

    c. Maintanance

    d. Maintenance

42. I didn't find it very _____.

    a. Humoros

    b. Humouros

    c. Humorous

    d. Humorus

43. She hasn't been here to my _____.

    a. Knowlege

    b. Knowledge

    c. Knowlegde

    d. Knowlledge

44. I never was very good at _____.

    a. Mathematics

    b. Mathmatics

    c. Matematics

    d. Mathamatics

45. I will look at it when I have some _____ time.

    a. Leisuire

    b. Lesure

    c. Lesure

    d. Leisure

46. Choose the phrase that is not spelled correctly.

    a. sufficeint resources

    b. collectible coins

    c. inconvenient truth

    d. fourth revision

47. Choose the phrase that is not spelled correctly.

    a. gothic cemetery

    b. magicaley disappear

    c. broccoli and cheese

    d. baked potatoes

48. Choose the phrase that is not spelled correctly.

    a. heavy equipmment

    b. English grammar

    c. weird sounds

    d. high intelligence

49. Choose the phrase that is not spelled correctly.

    a. foreign accent

    b. minature house

    c. mischievous elves

    d. changeable weather

50. Choose the phrase that is not spelled correctly.

    a. turn of the millennium

    b. sharp scissors

    c. disatrous outcome

    d. glass ceiling

Answer Key

Section 1 – Reading

1. B
We can infer from this passage that sickness from an infectious disease can be easily transmitted from one person to another.

From the passage, "Infectious pathologies are also called communicable diseases or transmissible diseases, due to their potential of transmission from one person or species to another by a replicating agent (as opposed to a toxin)."

2. A
Two other names for infectious pathologies are communicable diseases and transmissible diseases.

From the passage, "Infectious pathologies are also called communicable diseases or transmissible diseases, due to their potential of transmission from one person or species to another by a replicating agent (as opposed to a toxin)."

3. C
Infectivity describes the ability of an organism to enter, survive and multiply in the host. This is taken directly from the passage, and is a definition type question.

Definition type questions can be answered quickly and easily by scanning the passage for the word you are asked to define.

"Infectivity" is an unusual word, so it is quick and easy to scan the passage looking for this word.

4. B
We know an infection is not synonymous with an infectious disease because an infection may not cause important clinical symptoms or impair host function.

5. C
The purpose of this text is to explain when meteorologists consider a thunderstorm severe.

The main idea is the first sentence, "The United States National Weather Service classifies thunderstorms as severe when they reach a predetermined level." After the first sentence, the passage explains and elaborates on this idea. Everything is this passage is related to this idea, and there are no other major ideas in this passage that are central to the whole passage.

6. A
From this passage, we can infer that different areas and countries have different criteria for determining a severe storm.

From the passage we can see that most of the US has a criteria of, winds over 50 knots (58 mph or 93 km/h), and hail ¾ inch (2 cm). For the Central US, hail must be 1 inch (2.5 cm) in diameter. In Canada, winds must be 90 km/h or greater, hail 2 centimeters in diameter or greater, and rainfall more than 50 millimeters in 1 hour, or 75 millimeters in 3 hours.

Option D is incorrect because the Canadian system is the same for hail, 2 centimeters in diameter.

7. C
With hail above the minimum size of 2.5 cm. diameter, the Central Region of the United States National Weather Service would issue a severe thunderstorm warning.

8. C
You would find information about natural selection and adaptation in the ecology section which begins on page 110.

9. D
Clouds in space are made of different materials attracted by gravity. Clouds on Earth are made of water droplets or ice crystals.

Option D is the best answer. Notice also that option D is the most specific.

10. C

The main idea is the first sentence of the passage; a cloud is a visible mass of droplets or frozen crystals floating in the atmosphere above the surface of the Earth or other planetary body.

The main idea is very often the first sentence of the paragraph.

11. C

This question asks about the process, and gives options that can be confirmed or eliminated easily.

From the passage, "Dense, deep clouds reflect most light, so they appear white, at least from the top. Cloud droplets scatter light very efficiently, so the further into a cloud light travels, the weaker it gets. This accounts for the gray or dark appearance at the base of large clouds."

We can eliminate option A, since water droplets inside the cloud do not reflect light is false.

We can eliminate option B, since, water droplets outside the cloud reflect light, it appears dark, is false.

Option C is correct.

12. A

Secede most nearly means to break away from because the 11 states wanted to leave the United States and form their own country.

Option B is incorrect because the states were not accomplishing anything. Option C is incorrect because the states were trying to leave the USA not join it. Option D is incorrect because the states seceded before they lost the war.

13. B

Look at the dates in the passage. The shots were fired on April 12 and Congress declared war on April 14.

Option C is incorrect because the passage states that Lincoln was against slavery. Option D is incorrect because it never mentions who was or was not at Fort Sumter.

14. C
The passage states that Lee surrendered to Grant after the capture of the capital of the Confederacy, which is Richmond.

Option A is incorrect because the war continued for 2 years after Gettysburg. Option B is incorrect because that battle is not mentioned in the passage. Option D is incorrect because the capture of the capital occurred after the march to the sea.

15. A
When the passage said that the North had *abolished* slavery, it implies that slaves were no longer allowed in the North. In essence slavery was banned.

Option B makes no sense in relation to the context of the passage. Option C is incorrect because we know the North was fighting against slavery, not for it. Option D is incorrect because slavery is not a tangible thing that can be destroyed. It is a practice that had to be outlawed or banned.

16. A
Navy SEALS are the maritime component of the United States Special Operations Command (USSOCOM).

17. C
Working underwater separates SEALs from other military units. This is taken directly from the passage.

18. D
SEALs also belong to the Navy and the Coast Guard.

19. A
The CIA also participated. From the passage, the raid was conducted by a "team of 40 *CIA-led* Navy SEALS."

20. C
From the passage, "The Navy SEALs were part of the Naval Special Warfare Development Group, previously called

"Team 6". "

21. A
The sentence is a recommendation.

22. C
Tips for a good night's sleep is the best alternative title for this article.

23. B
Mental activity is helpful for a good night's sleep can not be inferred from this article.

24. A
The Save the Children's fund has raised $12,000 out of $20,000, or 12/20. Simplifying, 12/20 = 3/5

25. B
The Save the Children's fund has raised $12,000 out of $16,000, or 12/16. Simplifying, 12/16 = 3/4

Mathematics

1. D
75/1500 = 15/300 = 3/60 = 1/20

2. B
Estimate 215 X 65. First start with 200 X 50, which is 10,000, so the answer will be about 10,000. The only choice that is close is 13,500, option B.

3. B

Day	Number of Absent Students	Number of Present Students	% Attendance
Monday	5	40	88.88%
Tuesday	9	36	80.00%
Wednesday	4	41	91.11%
Thursday	10	35	77.77%
Friday	6	39	86.66%

88.88 + 80.00 + 91.11 + 77.77 + 86.66/5
424.42/5 = 84.88
Round up to 85%.

Percentage attendance will be 85%

4. D
First find a common denominator, 2/3 - 2/5 = 10 - 6 /15 =
4/15

5. C
0.27 + 0.33 = 0.60 and 0.60 = 60/100 = 3/5

6. B
(7 x 7 x 7 x 7 x 7) - (3 x 3 x 3 x 3 x 3) = 16,807 – 243 =
16,564

7. B
2/4 X 3/4 = 6/16, and lowest terms = 3/8

8. B
4y + 24 = 3y + 30
4y – 3y = 30 - 24
y = 6

9. B
2/3 x 60 = 40 and 1/5 x 75 = 15, 40 + 15 = 55.

10. A
1/3 X 3/4 = 3/12 = 1/4

11. D
3.13 + 7.87 = 11 and 11 X 5 = 55

12. A
5^6

13. C
Exponential form is 9^3 and standard from is 729

14. B
$(4)(3)^3 = (4)(27) = 108$

15. B
0.524/ 10 x 10 x 10 = 0.524/1000 = 0.000524

16. C
3x - 27 = 0
3x = 27
x = 9

17. C
First convert to decimal 7/11 = .63 and 5/7 = .714
2/3, option C (.667) is the only option between the two given
numbers.

18. B
0.25 + 0.65 = 0.9 = 9/10

19. C
 389 + 454 = 843

20. C
9,177 + 7,204 = 16,381

21. D
2,199 + 5,832 = 8,031

22. B
8,390 - 5,239 = 3,151

23. A
643 - 587 = 56

24. C
3,406 - 2,767 = 639

25. B
149 × 7 = 1043

Applied Mathematics

1. D
The formula for volume of a shape is L x W x H = 20 x 20 x 20 = 8,000 cm³

2. D
Let old salary = X, therefore $150 = x + 0.30x, 150 = 1x + 0.30x, 150 = 1.30x, x = 150/1.30 = 115.4

3. C
Cash = $75600. Building after one year = 80500 X 1.1 = $88550. Machinery after one year = 125000 X 0.8 = $100000. Total asset value = $264,150.

4. C
If there are 5 friends and each drink costs $1.89, we can round up to $2 per drink and estimate the total cost at, 5 X $2 = $10.

The actual cost is 5 X $1.89 = $9.45.

5. A
At 100% efficiency 1 machine produces 1450/10 = 145 m of cloth.
At 95% efficiency, 4 machines produce 4 X 0.95 X 145 = 551 m of cloth.
At 90% efficiency, 6 machines produce 6 X 0.90 X 145 = 783 m of cloth.

Total cloth produced = 145 + 551 + 783 = 1479m

6. A
The correct equation is X + 0.005xy.

7. A
The graph shows oil consumption peaked in 2011.

8. D
Total votes cast = 945 + 860 + 1210 = 3015
Total registered voters at all 3 polling stations =

1270 + 1050 + 1440 = 3760
Turnout = 3015/3760 = .802 X 100 = 80.186 or about 80%

9. B
Total expenses = 5284.34 + $8,384.76 + $2,920.00 =
16589.10

Profit = revenue less expenses

$19,304.56 - $16,589.10 = $2,715.46

10. D
If the lot is square, all sides are equal, so one side will be
$\sqrt{100}$ = 10. Area of a square is one side X one side = 10 X 10
= 100 sq. ft.

11. B
40% of 8.50 = 8.5 X .4 = $3.40. Including tips, $3.40 + 1.30
= $4.70

12. D
Taking Mr. Jones's total to calculate the price of an adult
ticket, 38.5/7 = 5.5. Mr. Jones bought 9 adult tickets for a
cost of 9 X 5.5 = $49.50.

Total cost was 67, so to calculate the cost of children's
ticket, 67 - 49.5 = 17.5. 17.5/5 = $3.50

13. C
Equilateral triangle with 9 cm. sides
Perimeter = 9 + 9 + 9 = 27 cm.

14. D
Perimeter of triangle ABC inside a rectangle.
Perimeter = 8.5 + 8.5 + 6 + 6
Perimeter = 29 cm.

15. B
She spent 15% - 100% - 15% = 85%

16. D
Formula for volume of a shape is L x W x H = 10 x 8 x 10 =
800 cm³

17. B
This is a compound interest problem. Calculate the interest earned in the first year and then use that total for the second year calculation.

In the first year, 5000 X .04 = 200
In the second year, 5200 X .04 = 208
Total at the end of the second year = $5408

18. B
His distribution is like that
300 kg -> 20 × 15 -> 6.4×15 = $96
120 kg -> 10 × 12 -> 3.4×12 = $40.8
130 kg -> 5 × 26 -> 1.8×26 = $46.8

Total will be = $183.6
Deducing distribution cost, his net profit will be
183.6 - 175 = $13.6

19. D
The distance covered by the car = 60 X 3.5 = 210 km. Time required by the motorbike = 210/40 = 5.25 hr.

20. D
The number is 51.738. The last digit is greater than 5, so it is removed and 1 is added to the next number to the left. Answer = 51.74.

21. C
The ratio between gold, silver and bronze coins is 2:6:8. Bring to the lowest terms by dividing each side by 2 gives 1:3:4.

22. B
The line is pointing towards numbers less than 1. The equation is therefore, X < 1.

23. A
The line is pointing towards numbers greater than 2. The equation is therefore, X < 2.

24. C
The decimal point moves 9 spaces right to be placed after 7,

which is the first non-zero number. Thus 7.892×10^9

25. D
Each time the * and + alternate, either singly or doubles.

English

1. D
Use an exclamation mark after an imperative sentence if the command is urgent and forceful.

2. A
A comma is used before the conjunction to separate two independent clauses in a compound sentence.

3. C
A semicolon is also used to join two clauses that present a direct contrast. In this question, the sentence has two extremes in a similar situation. Notice that even when the two clauses present a contrast, the subjects of the two clauses are similar.

4. C
A semi colon may also be used to prevent confusion. The other obvious choice is this sentence would be a comma, but it isn't an option.

5. A
A comma is used to separate three or more words, phrases or clauses in a series.

6. C
The semicolon links independent clauses.

7. A
The semicolon links independent clauses with a conjunction (However).

8. B
The semicolon links independent clauses.

9. D
A colon informs the reader that what follows the mark proves, explains, or lists elements of what preceded the

mark.

10. A
A colon informs the reader that what follows the mark proves, explains, or lists elements of what preceded the mark.

11. A
Option A is the only option that includes quotation marks around the quoted speech and a question mark.

12. A
In option A, "city" is capitalized because it is use in the phrase, "City of Miami." "Florida" in this sentence is also correctly capitalized. Option B does not capitalize "Florida." Option C omits an apostrophe in "California's best beaches." Option D does not capitalize "Brooklyn."

13. B
Option A has incorrect capitalization of "Wall Street Journal." The names of publications are capitalized. Option C incorrect capitalizes "Weekend Newspaper." Option D incorrectly capitalizes "USA Today."

14. D
Option A uses commas incorrectly. Option B uses both commas and capitalization incorrectly, and option D uses a dash where it is not required.

15. A
Option A correctly capitalizes the singers name, includes the name of the song in quotes, as well as capitalizes "Grammys." Option B does not include the name of the song in quotes. Option C incorrectly uses dashes, and option D incorrectly uses quotation marks.

16. C
17. A
18. B
19. D
20. A
21. C
22. C
23. C

24. D

25. B

26. D

The sentence is correct. The other options add an additional and unnecessary comma.

27. A

"Equipt" is incorrect - the correct form is "equipped with."

28. D

The phrase, "function of some insects" is singular, so "is" is correct.

29. C

The correct usage for comparing two things is "difference between."

30. A

Option A uses the contraction "it's" correctly.

Vocabulary

31. C

Veterinarian: a person qualified to treat diseased or injured animals.

32. A

Immune: resistant to a particular virus or toxin.

33. D

Pesticide: a substance used for destroying insects or other organisms harmful to cultivated plants or to animals.

34. A

Famine: extreme scarcity of food.

35. B

Hormones: a regulatory substance produced in an organism and transported in tissue fluids such as blood or sap to stimulate specific cells or tissues into action.

36. A

Maverick: Showing independence in thoughts or actions.

37. C
Pandemonium: wild and noisy disorder or confusion; up-roar.

38. B
Dissipate: disperse or scatter.

39. A
Gaunt: lean and haggard, esp. because of suffering, hunger, or age.

40. B
Remuneration: A payment for work done; wages, salary.

Spelling

41. D
Maintenance is the correct spelling.

42. C
Humorous is the correct spelling.

43. B
Knowledge is the correct spelling.

44. A
Mathematics is the correct spelling.

45. D
Leisure is the correct spelling.

46. A
Sufficeint is incorrect. The correct spelling is sufficient.

47. B
Magicaley is incorrect. The correct spelling is magically.

48. A
Equipmment is incorrect. The correct spelling is equipment.

49. B
Minature is incorrect. The correct spelling is miniature.

50. C
Disatrous is incorrect. The correct spelling is disastrous.

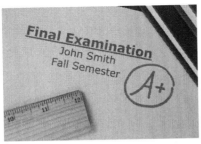

Practice Test Questions Set 2

The practice test portion presents questions that are representative of the type of question you should expect to find on the TABE®. However, they are not intended to match exactly what is on the TABE®.

For the best results, take this Practice Test as if it were the real exam. Set aside time when you will not be disturbed, and a location that is quiet and free of distractions. Read the instructions carefully, read each question carefully, and answer to the best of your ability.

Use the bubble answer sheets provided. When you have completed the Practice Test, check your answer against the Answer Key and read the explanation provided.

Reading

1. Ⓐ Ⓑ Ⓒ Ⓓ   11. Ⓐ Ⓑ Ⓒ Ⓓ   21. Ⓐ Ⓑ Ⓒ Ⓓ

2. Ⓐ Ⓑ Ⓒ Ⓓ   12. Ⓐ Ⓑ Ⓒ Ⓓ   22. Ⓐ Ⓑ Ⓒ Ⓓ

3. Ⓐ Ⓑ Ⓒ Ⓓ   13. Ⓐ Ⓑ Ⓒ Ⓓ   23. Ⓐ Ⓑ Ⓒ Ⓓ

4. Ⓐ Ⓑ Ⓒ Ⓓ   14. Ⓐ Ⓑ Ⓒ Ⓓ   24. Ⓐ Ⓑ Ⓒ Ⓓ

5. Ⓐ Ⓑ Ⓒ Ⓓ   15. Ⓐ Ⓑ Ⓒ Ⓓ   25. Ⓐ Ⓑ Ⓒ Ⓓ

6. Ⓐ Ⓑ Ⓒ Ⓓ   16. Ⓐ Ⓑ Ⓒ Ⓓ

7. Ⓐ Ⓑ Ⓒ Ⓓ   17. Ⓐ Ⓑ Ⓒ Ⓓ

8. Ⓐ Ⓑ Ⓒ Ⓓ   18. Ⓐ Ⓑ Ⓒ Ⓓ

9. Ⓐ Ⓑ Ⓒ Ⓓ   19. Ⓐ Ⓑ Ⓒ Ⓓ

10. Ⓐ Ⓑ Ⓒ Ⓓ   20. Ⓐ Ⓑ Ⓒ Ⓓ

Computational Mathematics

1. Ⓐ Ⓑ Ⓒ Ⓓ   11. Ⓐ Ⓑ Ⓒ Ⓓ   21. Ⓐ Ⓑ Ⓒ Ⓓ

2. Ⓐ Ⓑ Ⓒ Ⓓ   12. Ⓐ Ⓑ Ⓒ Ⓓ   22. Ⓐ Ⓑ Ⓒ Ⓓ

3. Ⓐ Ⓑ Ⓒ Ⓓ   13. Ⓐ Ⓑ Ⓒ Ⓓ   23. Ⓐ Ⓑ Ⓒ Ⓓ

4. Ⓐ Ⓑ Ⓒ Ⓓ   14. Ⓐ Ⓑ Ⓒ Ⓓ   24. Ⓐ Ⓑ Ⓒ Ⓓ

5. Ⓐ Ⓑ Ⓒ Ⓓ   15. Ⓐ Ⓑ Ⓒ Ⓓ   25. Ⓐ Ⓑ Ⓒ Ⓓ

6. Ⓐ Ⓑ Ⓒ Ⓓ   16. Ⓐ Ⓑ Ⓒ Ⓓ

7. Ⓐ Ⓑ Ⓒ Ⓓ   17. Ⓐ Ⓑ Ⓒ Ⓓ

8. Ⓐ Ⓑ Ⓒ Ⓓ   18. Ⓐ Ⓑ Ⓒ Ⓓ

9. Ⓐ Ⓑ Ⓒ Ⓓ   19. Ⓐ Ⓑ Ⓒ Ⓓ

10. Ⓐ Ⓑ Ⓒ Ⓓ   20. Ⓐ Ⓑ Ⓒ Ⓓ

Applied Mathematics

1. Ⓐ Ⓑ Ⓒ Ⓓ   11. Ⓐ Ⓑ Ⓒ Ⓓ   21. Ⓐ Ⓑ Ⓒ Ⓓ

2. Ⓐ Ⓑ Ⓒ Ⓓ   12. Ⓐ Ⓑ Ⓒ Ⓓ   22. Ⓐ Ⓑ Ⓒ Ⓓ

3. Ⓐ Ⓑ Ⓒ Ⓓ   13. Ⓐ Ⓑ Ⓒ Ⓓ   23. Ⓐ Ⓑ Ⓒ Ⓓ

4. Ⓐ Ⓑ Ⓒ Ⓓ   14. Ⓐ Ⓑ Ⓒ Ⓓ   24. Ⓐ Ⓑ Ⓒ Ⓓ

5. Ⓐ Ⓑ Ⓒ Ⓓ   15. Ⓐ Ⓑ Ⓒ Ⓓ   25. Ⓐ Ⓑ Ⓒ Ⓓ

6. Ⓐ Ⓑ Ⓒ Ⓓ   16. Ⓐ Ⓑ Ⓒ Ⓓ

7. Ⓐ Ⓑ Ⓒ Ⓓ   17. Ⓐ Ⓑ Ⓒ Ⓓ

8. Ⓐ Ⓑ Ⓒ Ⓓ   18. Ⓐ Ⓑ Ⓒ Ⓓ

9. Ⓐ Ⓑ Ⓒ Ⓓ   19. Ⓐ Ⓑ Ⓒ Ⓓ

10. Ⓐ Ⓑ Ⓒ Ⓓ   20. Ⓐ Ⓑ Ⓒ Ⓓ

Language

1. Ⓐ Ⓑ Ⓒ Ⓓ   11. Ⓐ Ⓑ Ⓒ Ⓓ   21. Ⓐ Ⓑ Ⓒ Ⓓ   31. Ⓐ Ⓑ Ⓒ Ⓓ

2. Ⓐ Ⓑ Ⓒ Ⓓ   12. Ⓐ Ⓑ Ⓒ Ⓓ   22. Ⓐ Ⓑ Ⓒ Ⓓ   32. Ⓐ Ⓑ Ⓒ Ⓓ

3. Ⓐ Ⓑ Ⓒ Ⓓ   13. Ⓐ Ⓑ Ⓒ Ⓓ   23. Ⓐ Ⓑ Ⓒ Ⓓ   33. Ⓐ Ⓑ Ⓒ Ⓓ

4. Ⓐ Ⓑ Ⓒ Ⓓ   14. Ⓐ Ⓑ Ⓒ Ⓓ   24. Ⓐ Ⓑ Ⓒ Ⓓ   34. Ⓐ Ⓑ Ⓒ Ⓓ

5. Ⓐ Ⓑ Ⓒ Ⓓ   15. Ⓐ Ⓑ Ⓒ Ⓓ   25. Ⓐ Ⓑ Ⓒ Ⓓ   35. Ⓐ Ⓑ Ⓒ Ⓓ

6. Ⓐ Ⓑ Ⓒ Ⓓ   16. Ⓐ Ⓑ Ⓒ Ⓓ   26. Ⓐ Ⓑ Ⓒ Ⓓ   36. Ⓐ Ⓑ Ⓒ Ⓓ

7. Ⓐ Ⓑ Ⓒ Ⓓ   17. Ⓐ Ⓑ Ⓒ Ⓓ   27. Ⓐ Ⓑ Ⓒ Ⓓ   37. Ⓐ Ⓑ Ⓒ Ⓓ

8. Ⓐ Ⓑ Ⓒ Ⓓ   18. Ⓐ Ⓑ Ⓒ Ⓓ   28. Ⓐ Ⓑ Ⓒ Ⓓ   38. Ⓐ Ⓑ Ⓒ Ⓓ

9. Ⓐ Ⓑ Ⓒ Ⓓ   19. Ⓐ Ⓑ Ⓒ Ⓓ   29. Ⓐ Ⓑ Ⓒ Ⓓ   39. Ⓐ Ⓑ Ⓒ Ⓓ

10. Ⓐ Ⓑ Ⓒ Ⓓ   20. Ⓐ Ⓑ Ⓒ Ⓓ   30. Ⓐ Ⓑ Ⓒ Ⓓ   40. Ⓐ Ⓑ Ⓒ Ⓓ

Reading and Language Arts

Questions 1 - 4 refer to the following passage.

Was Dr. Seuss A Real Doctor?

A favorite author for over 100 years, Theodor Seuss Geisel was born on March 2, 1902. Today, we celebrate the birthday of the famous "Dr. Seuss" by hosting Read Across America events throughout the month of March. School children around the country celebrate the "Doctor's" birthday by making hats, giving presentations and holding read aloud circles featuring some of Dr. Seuss' most famous books.

But who was Dr. Seuss? Did he go to medical school? Where was his office? You may be surprised to know that Theodor Seuss Geisel was not a medical doctor at all. He took on the nickname Dr. Seuss when he became a noted children's book author. He earned the nickname because people said his books were "as good as medicine". All these years later, his nickname has lasted and he is known as Dr. Seuss all across the world.

Think back to when you were a young child. Did you ever want to try "green eggs and ham."? Did you try to "Hop on Pop"? Do you remember learning about the environment from a creature called The Lorax? Of course, you must recall one of Seuss' most famous characters; that green Grinch who stole Christmas. These stories were all written by Dr. Seuss and featured his signature rhyming words and letters. They also featured made up words in order to enhance his rhyme scheme and even though many of his characters were made up, they sure seem real to us today.

And what of his "signature" book, The Cat in the Hat? You must remember that cat and Thing One and Thing Two from your childhood. Did you know that in the early 1950's there was a growing concern in America that children were not becoming avid readers? This was, book publishers thought, because children found books dull and uninteresting. An intelligent publisher sent Dr. Seuss a book of words that he thought all children should learn as young readers. Dr. Seuss wrote his famous story The Cat in the Hat, using those words. We can see, over the decades, just how much influence his writing has had on very young children. That is why we celebrate this doctor's birthday each March.

1. What does the word "avid" mean in the last paragraph?

    a. Good

    b. Interested

    c. Slow

    d. Fast

2. What can we infer from the statement " His books were like medicine"?

    a. His books made people feel better

    b. His books were in doctor's office waiting rooms

    c. His books took away fevers

    d. His books left a funny taste in readers' mouths.

3. Why is the publisher in the last paragraph referred to as "intelligent?"

    a. The publisher knew how to read.

    b. The publisher knew kids did not like to read.

    c. The publisher knew Dr. Seuss would be able to create a book that sold well.

    d. The publisher knew that Dr. Seuss would be able to write a book that would get young children interested in reading.

4. The theme of this passage is

a. Dr. Seuss was not a doctor.

b. Dr. Seuss influenced the lives of generations of young children.

c. Dr. Seuss wrote rhyming books.

d. Dr. Suess' birthday is a good day to read a book.

Questions 5 - 8 refer to the following passage.

Low Blood Sugar

As the name suggest, low blood sugar is low sugar levels in the bloodstream. This can occur when you have not eaten properly and undertake strenuous activity, or when you are very hungry. When Low blood sugar occurs regularly and is ongoing, it is a medical condition called hypoglycemia. This condition can occur in diabetics and also in healthy adults.

Causes of low blood sugar can include excessive alcohol consumption, metabolic problems, stomach surgery, pancreas, liver or kidneys problems, as well as a side-effect of some medications.

Symptoms

There are different symptoms depending on the severity of the case.

Mild hypoglycemia can lead to feelings of nausea and hunger. The patient may also feel nervous, jittery and have fast heart beats. Sweaty skin, clammy and cold skin are likely symptoms.

Moderate hypoglycemia can result in a short temper, confusion, nervousness, fear and blurring of vision. The patient may feel weak and unsteady.

Severe cases of hypoglycemia can lead to seizures, coma, fainting spells, nightmares, headaches, excessive sweats and severe tiredness.

Diagnosis of low blood sugar

A doctor can diagnosis this medical condition by asking the patient questions and testing blood and urine samples. Home testing kits are available for patients to monitor blood sugar levels. It is important to see a qualified doctor though. The doctor can administer tests to ensure that will safely rule out other medical conditions that could affect blood sugar levels.

Treatment

Quick treatments include drinking or eating foods and drinks with high sugar contents. Good examples include soda, fruit juice, hard candy and raisins. Glucose energy tablets can also help. Doctors may also recommend medications and well as changes in diet and exercise routine to treat chronic low blood sugar.

5. Based on the article, which of the following is true?

a. Low blood sugar can happen to anyone.

b. Low blood sugar only happens to diabetics.

c. Low blood sugar can occur even.

d. None of the statements are true.

6. Which of the following are the author's opinion?

a. Quick treatments include drinking or eating foods and drinks with high sugar contents.

b. None of the statements are opinions.

c. This condition can occur in diabetics and also in healthy adults.

d. There are different symptoms depending on the severity of the case

7. What is the author's purpose?

    a. To inform

    b. To persuade

    c. To entertain

    d. To analyze

8. Which of the following is not a detail?

    a. A doctor can diagnosis this medical condition by asking the patient questions and testing.

    b. A doctor will test blood and urine samples.

    c. Glucose energy tablets can also help.

    d. Home test kits monitor blood sugar levels.

Questions 9 - 12 refer to the following passage.

Who Was Anne Frank?

You may have heard mention of the word Holocaust in your History or English classes. The Holocaust took place from 1939-1945. It was an attempt by the Nazi party to purify the human race, by eliminating Jews, Gypsies, Catholics, homosexuals and others they deemed inferior to their "perfect" Aryan race. The Nazis used Concentration Camps, which were sometimes used as Death Camps, in order to exterminate the people they held in the camps. One of the saddest facts about the Holocaust was the over one million children under the age of sixteen died in a Nazi concentration camp. Just a few weeks before World War II was over, Anne Frank was one of those children to die.

Before the Nazi party began its persecution of the Jews, Anne Frank had a happy live. She was born in June of 1929. In June of 1942, for her 13th birthday, she was given a simple present which would go on to impact the lives of millions of people around the world. That gift was a small red diary that she called Kitty. This diary was to become Anne's most treasured possession when she and her family hid from the Nazi's in a secret annex above her father's office building in Amsterdam.

For 25 months, Anne, her sister Margot, her parents, another family, and an elderly Jewish dentist hid from the Nazis in this tiny annex. They were never permitted to go outside and their food and supplies were brought to them by Miep Gies and her husband, who did not believe in the Nazi persecution of the Jews. It was a very difficult life for young Anne and she used Kitty as an outlet to describe her life in hiding. After 2 years, Anne and her family were betrayed and arrested by the Nazis. To this day, nobody is exactly sure who betrayed the Frank family and the other annex residents. Anne, her mother, and her sister were separated from Otto Frank, Anne's father. Then, Anne and Margot were separated from their mother. In March of 1945, Margot Frank died of starvation in a Concentration Camp. A few days later, at the age of 15, Anne Frank died of typhus. Of all the people who hid in the Annex, only Otto Frank survived the Holocaust.

Otto Frank returned to the Annex after World War II. It was there that he found Kitty, filled with Anne's thoughts and feelings about being a persecuted Jewish girl. Otto Frank had Anne's diary published in 1947 and it has remained continuously in print ever since. Today, the diary has been published in over 55 languages and more than 24 million copies have been sold around the world. The Diary of Anne Frank tells the story of a brave young woman who tried to see the good in all people.

9. From the context clues in the passage, the word Annex most nearly means?

    a. Attic

    b. Bedroom

    c. Basement

    d. Kitchen

10. Why do you think Anne's diary has been published in 55 languages?

a. So everyone could understand it.

b. So people around the world could learn more about the horrors of the Holocaust.

c. Because Anne was Jewish but hid in Amsterdam and died in Germany.

d. Because Otto Frank spoke many languages.

11. From the description of Anne and Margot's deaths in the passage, what can we assume typhus is?

a. The same as starving to death.

b. An infection the Germans gave to Anne.

c. A disease Anne caught in the concentration camp.

d. Poison gas used by the Germans to kill Anne.

12. In the third paragraph, what does the word outlet most nearly mean?

a. A place to plug things into the wall

b. A store where Miep bought cheap supplies for the Frank family

c. A hiding space similar to an Annex

d. A place where Anne could express her private thoughts.

Questions 13 - 16 refer to the following passage.

Myths, Legend and Folklore

Cultural historians draw a distinction between myth, legend and folktale simply as a way to group traditional stories. However, in many cultures, drawing a sharp line between myths and legends is not that simple. Instead of dividing their traditional stories into myths, legends, and folktales, some cultures divide them into two categories. The first category roughly corresponds to folktales, and the second is one that combines myths and legends. Similarly, we can not always separate myths from folktales. One society might consider a story true, making it a myth. Another society may believe the story is fiction, which makes it a folktale. In fact, when a myth loses its status as part of a religious system, it often takes on traits more typical of folktales, with its formerly divine characters now appearing as human heroes, giants, or fairies. Myth, legend, and folktale are only a few of the categories of traditional stories. Other categories include anecdotes and some kinds of jokes. Traditional stories, in turn, are only one category within the much larger category of folklore, which also includes items such as gestures, costumes, and music. [7]

13. The main idea of this passage is that

a. Myths, fables, and folktales are not the same thing, and each describes a specific type of story

b. Traditional stories can be categorized in different ways by different people

c. Cultures use myths for religious purposes, and when this is no longer true, the people forget and discard these myths

d. Myths can never become folk tales, because one is true, and the other is false

14. The terms myth and legend are

a. Categories that are synonymous with true and false

b. Categories that group traditional stories according to certain characteristics

c. Interchangeable, because both terms mean a story that is passed down from generation to generation

d. Meant to distinguish between a story that involves a hero and a cultural message and a story meant only to entertain

15. Traditional story categories not only include myths and legends, but

 a. Can also include gestures, since some cultures passed these down before the written and spoken word

 b. In addition, folklore refers to stories involving fables and fairy tales

 c. These story categories can also include folk music and traditional dress

 d. Traditional stories themselves are a part of the larger category of folklore, which may also include costumes, gestures, and music

16. This passage shows that

 a. There is a distinct difference between a myth and a legend, although both are folktales

 b. Myths are folktales, but folktales are not myths

 c. Myths, legends, and folktales play an important part in tradition and the past, and are a rich and colorful part of history

 d. Most cultures consider myths to be true

Questions 17 - 20 refer to the following passage.

What Is Mardi Gras?

Mardi Gras is fast becoming one of the South's most famous and most celebrated holidays. The word Mardi Gras comes from the French and the literal translation is "Fat Tuesday". The holiday has also been called Shrove Tuesday, due to its associations with Lent. The purpose of Mardi Gras is to celebrate and enjoy before the Lenten season of fasting and repentance begins.

What originated by the French Explorers in New Orleans, Louisiana in the 17th century is now celebrated all over the world. Panama, Italy, Belgium and Brazil all host large scale Mardi Gras celebrations, and many smaller cities and towns celebrate this fun loving Tuesday as well. Usually held in February or early March, Mardi Gras is a day of extravagance, a day for people to eat, drink and be merry, to wear costumes, masks and to dance to jazz music.

The French explorers on the Mississippi River would be in shock today if they saw the opulence of the parades and floats that grace the New Orleans streets during Mardi Gras these days. Parades in New Orleans are divided by organizations. These are more commonly known as Krewes.

Being a member of a Krewe is quite a task because Krewes are responsible for overseeing the parades. Each Krewe's parade is ruled by a Mardi Gras "King and Queen". The role of the King and Queen is to "bestow" gifts on their adoring fans as the floats ride along the street. They throw doubloons, which is fake money and usually colored green, purple and gold, which are the colors of Mardi Gras. Beads in those color shades are also thrown and cups are thrown as well. Beads are by far the most popular souvenir of any Mardi Gras parade, with each spectator attempting to gather as many as possible.

17. The purpose of Mardi Gras is to

    a. Repent for a month.

    b. Celebrate in extravagant ways.

    c. Be a member of a Krewe.

    d. Explore the Mississippi.

18. From reading the passage we can infer that "Kings and Queens"

    a. Have to be members of a Krewe.

    b. Have to be French.

    c. Have to know how to speak French.

    d. Have to give away their own money.

19. Which group of people first began to hold Mardi Gras celebrations?

    a. Settlers from Italy

    b. Members of Krewes

    c. French explorers

    d. Belgium explorers

20. In the context of the passage, what does the word spectator most nearly mean?

    a. Someone who participates actively

    b. Someone who watches the parade's action

    c. Someone on one of the parade floats

    d. Someone who does not celebrate Mardi Gras

Questions 21 - 22 refer to the following passage.

Thunderstorms

Warm air is less dense than cool air, so warm air rises within cooler air like a hot air balloon or warm water in an ocean current. Clouds form as warm air carrying moisture rises. As the warm air rises, it cools. The moist water vapor begins to condense as the temperature cools. This releases energy that keeps the air warmer than its surroundings. The result is that it continues to rise. If enough instability is present in the atmosphere, this process will continue long enough for cumulonimbus clouds to form. These clouds support lightning and thunder. All thunderstorms, regardless of type, go through three stages: the cumulus stage, the mature stage, and the dissipation stage. Depending on the conditions in the atmosphere, these three stages can take anywhere from 20 minutes to several hours. [5]

21. This passage tells us:

   a. Warm air is denser than cool air

   b. All thunderstorms will go through three stages.

   c. Thunderstorms may occur without clouds present.

   d. The stages of a thunderstorm conclude within just a few minutes.

22. What is the correct order?

   a. Warm air rises, cools as it gets higher, water condenses, warms the air, and the air rises more.

   b. Warm air rises, warms up more as it get higher, water condenses, warms the air, and the air rises more.

   c. Warm air rises, cools as it gets higher, water condenses, cools the air, and the air rises more.

   d. None of the above.

Questions 23 - 25 refer to the following passage.

The Life of Helen Keller

Many people have heard of Helen Keller. She is quite famous because she was unable to see or hear, but learned to speak and read and went on to attend college and earn a degree. Her life is a very interesting story, one that she developed into an autobiography, which was then adapted into both a stage play and a movie. How did Helen Keller overcome her disabilities to become a famous woman? Read on to find out.

Helen Keller was not born blind and deaf. When she was a small baby, she had a very high fever for several days. As a result of her sudden illness, baby Helen lost her eyesight and her hearing. Because she was so young when she went deaf and blind, Helen Keller never had any recollection of being able to see or hear. Since she could not hear, she could not learn to talk. Since she could not see, it was difficult for her to move around. For the first six years of her life, her world was very still and dark.

Imagine what Helen's childhood must have been like. She could not hear her mother's voice. She could not see the beauty of her parent's farm. She could not recognize who was giving her a hug, or a bath or even where her bedroom was each night. More sad, she could not communicate with her parents in any way. She could not express her feelings or tell them the things she wanted. It must have been a very sad childhood.

When Helen was six years old, her parents hired her a teacher named Anne Sullivan. Anne was a young woman who was almost blind. However, she could hear and she could read Braille, so she was a perfect teacher for young Helen. At first, Anne had a very hard time teaching Helen anything. She described her first impression of Helen as a "wild thing, not a child." Helen did not like Anne at first either. She bit and hit Anne when Anne tried to teach her. However, the two of them eventually came to have a great deal of love and respect for each other.

Anne taught Helen to hear by putting her hands on people's throats. She could feel the sounds that people made. In time, Helen learned to feel what people said. Next, Anne taught Helen to read Braille, which is a way that books are written for the blind. Finally, Anne taught Helen to talk. Although Helen did learn to talk, it was hard for anyone but Anne to understand her.

As Helen grew older, more and more people were amazed by her story. She went to college and wrote books about her life. She gave talks to the public, with Anne at her side, translating her words. Today, both Anne Sullivan and Helen Keller are famous women who are respected for their lives' work.

23. Helen Keller could not see and hear and so, her biggest problem in child hood was her inability to do what?

    a. Communicate

    b. Walk

    c. Play

    d. Eat

24. Helen learned to hear by feeling the vibrations people made when they spoke. What were these vibrations were felt through?

    a. Mouth

    b. Throat

    c. Ears

    d. Lips

25. From the passage, we can infer that Anne Sullivan was a patient teacher. We can infer this because

    a. Helen hit and bit her and Anne still remained her teacher.

    b. Anne taught Helen to read only.

    c. Anne was hard of hearing too.

    d. Anne wanted to be a teacher.

Computational Mathematics

1. 8974 – 8256 =

    a. 715

    b. 716

    c. 718

    d. 715

2. 4404 / 8 =

    a. 550.5

    b. 550

    c. 505

    d. 555

3. 274 * 139 =

a. 38006
b. 38860
c. 38060
d. 38086

4. 3567 + 99 =

a. 3066
b. 3666
c. 3606
d. 4666

5. Translate the following into an equation:

2 plus a number divided by 7.

a. $(2 + X)/7$
b. $(7 + X)/2$
c. $(2 + 7)/X$
d. $2/(7 + X)$

6. 60 is 75% of x. Solve for x.

a. 80
b. 90
c. 75
d. 70

7. Express 71/1000 as a decimal.

a. .71
b. .0071
c. .071
d. 7.1

8. .33 × .59 =

    a. .1947

    b. 1.95

    c. .0197

    d. .1817

9. 7x – 9 = 47. Solve for x.

    a. 8

    b. 7

    c. 9

    d. 6

10. What number is in the ten thousandths place in 1.7389

    a. 1

    b. 8

    c. 9

    d. 3

11. .87 - .48 =

    a. .39

    b. .49

    c. .41

    d. .37

12. Which is the equivalent decimal number for forty nine thousandths?

    a. .49

    b. .0049

    c. .049

    d. 4.9

13. Which of the following is not a fraction equivalent to 3/4?

    a. 6/8

    b. 9/12

    c. 12/18

    d. 21/28

14. Which one of the following is less than a third?

    a. 84/231

    b. 6/35

    c. 3/22

    d. b and c

15. Which of the following numbers is the greatest?

    a. 1

    b. $\sqrt{2}$

    c. 3/2

    d. 4/3

16. $2b + 9b - 5b = 0$

    a. 3b

    b. 6b

    c. 4b

    d. 8b

17. 4.7 + .9 + .01 =

    a. 5.5

    b. 6.51

    c. 5.61

    d. 5.7

18. 60% of x is 12. Solve for x.

   a. 18
   b. 15
   c. 25
   d. 20

19. .84 ÷ .7 =

   a. .12
   b. 12
   c. .012
   d. 1.2

20. 4120 – 3216 =

   a. 903
   b. 804
   c. 904
   d. 1904

21. 2417 + 1004 =

   a. 3401
   b. 4321
   c. 3402
   d. 3421

22. Simplify 0.12 + 1 2/5 – 1 3/5

   a. 1 1/25
   b. 1 3/25
   c. 1 2/5
   d. 2 3/5

23. What is the difference between 700,653 and 70,099?

    a. 4607854

    b. 5460

    c. 700765

    d. 630,0554

24. Simplify 0.25 + 1/3 + 2/3

    a. 1 1/4

    b. 2 1/4

    c. 1 1/3

    d. 2 1/4

25. Add 10% of 300 to 50% of 20

    a. 50

    b. 40

    c. 60

    d. 45

Applied Mathematics

1. If a train travels at 72 kilometers per hour, how far will it travel in 12 seconds?

    a. 200m

    b. 220m

    c. 240m

    d. 260m

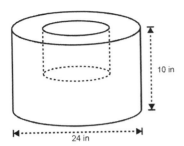

2. What is the volume of the above solid made by a hollow cylinder half the size of the larger cylinder?

   a. $1440 \, \pi \, \text{in}^3$

   b. $1260 \, \pi \, \text{in}^3$

   c. $1040 \, \pi \, \text{in}^3$

   d. $960 \, \pi \, \text{in}^3$

3. Tony bought 15 dozen eggs for $80. 16 eggs were broken during loading and unloading. He sold the remaining eggs for $0.54 each. What will be his percent profit?

   a. 11.25%

   b. 11.20%

   c. 11.50%

   d. 12%

4. In a class of 83 students, 72 are present. What percent of students are absent?

   a. 12%

   b. 13%

   c. 14%

   d. 15%

5. A student deposits $200 in a savings account hoping to buy a bicycle worth $245. If the bank offers a 15% interest rate, how long will she have to wait?

    a. 1½ years

    b. 2 ½ years

    c. 2 years

    d. 1 year

6. A man earns $600 as interest after 2 years of depositing a certain amount in a local bank. If the interest rate was 3%, how much was the original amount deposited?

    a. $3,600

    b. $100,000

    c. $10,000

    d. $1,000

Consider the following graph.

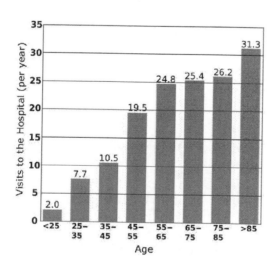

7. How many hospital visits per year does a person aged 85 or older make?

    a. 26.2

    b. 31.3

    c. More than 31.3

    d. A decision cannot be made from this graph.

8. Based on this graph, how many visits per year do you expect a person that is 95 or older to make?

    a. More than 31.3

    b. Less than 31.3

    c. 31.3

    d. A decision cannot be made from this graph.

9. How much water can be stored in a cylindrical container 5 meters in diameter and 12 meters high?

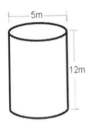

    a. 235.65 m^3

    b. 223.65 m^3

    c. 240.65 m^3

    d. 252.65 m^3

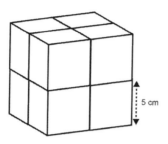

10. What is the volume of the figure above?

    a. 125 cm^3

    b. 875 cm^3

    c. 1000 cm^3

    d. 500 cm^3

11. Choose the expression the figure represents.

    a. X > 2

    b. X $\geq$ 2

    c. X < 2

    d. X $\leq$ 2

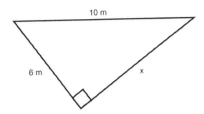

12. What is the length of the missing side in the triangle above?

    a. 6

    b. 4

    c. 8

    d. 5

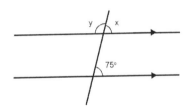

13. What is the value of the angle y?

    a. 25°

    b. 15°

    c. 30°

    d. 105°

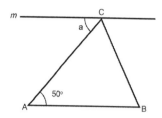

14. If the line *m* is parallel to the side AB of △ABC, what is angle *a*?

    a. 130°

    b. 25°

    c. 65°

    d. 50°

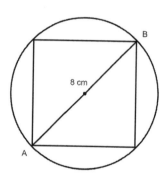

15. What is area of the circle?

    a. 4 π cm²

    b. 12 π cm²

    c. 10 π cm²

    d. 16 π cm²

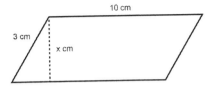

16. What is the perimeter of the parallelogram above?

a. 12 cm

b. 26 cm

c. 13 cm

d. (13+x) cm

17. Express 87% as a decimal.

a. .087

b. 8.7

c. .87

d. 87

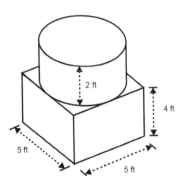

18. What is the approximate total volume of the above solid?

a. 120 ft³

b. 100 ft³

c. 140 ft³

d. 160 ft³

19. Susan wants to buy a leather jacket that costs $545.00 and is on sale for 10% off. What is the approximate cost?

    a. $525

    b. $450

    c. $475

    d. $500

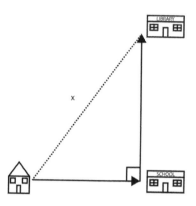

20. Every day starting from his home Peter travels due east 3 kilometers to the school. After school he travels due north 4 kilometers to the library. What is the distance between Peter's home and the library?

    a. 15 km

    b. 10 km

    c. 5 km

    d. 12 ½ km

21. If Tim deposits $5,500 in a savings account that offers a 5% interest, what will be the total amount in his savings account after 3 years?

    a. $6,225

    b. $6,0325

    c. $325

    d. $6,325

22. The cost of waterproofing canvas is .50 per square yard. What is the total cost for waterproofing a canvas truck cover that is 15' x 24'?

    a. $18.00

    b. $6.67

    c. $180.00

    d. $20.00

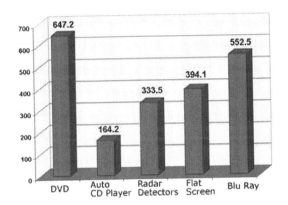

23. Consider the graph above. What is the third best-selling product?

    a. Radar Detectors

    b. Flat Screen TV

    c. Blu Ray

    d. Auto CD Players

24. Which two products are the closest in the number of sales?

    a. Blu Ray and Flat Screen TV

    b. Flat Screen TV and Radar Detectors

    c. Radar Detectors and Auto CD Players

    d. DVD players and Blu Ray

25. A small business owner deposits $6000 in a savings account at a local bank. After 2 years, at 3% interest rate, what will be the interest earned?

    a. $6360

    b. $360

    c. $240

    d. $460

Language

Directions: Fill in the blank with the correct punctuation.

1. The recipe requires the following ingredients _____ flour, sugar, eggs, baking powder and vanilla.

    a. ,

    b. :

    c. ;

    d. .

2. Lindsay said _____ "It's a beautiful day."

    a. ,

    b. :

    c. ;

    d. .

3. Dear Ms. Smith___

    a. :

    b. ,

    c. .

    d. !

4. Her sister____s bag was full of useless items

    a. " "
    b. '
    c. ,
    d. –

5. Actors try to empathize with ___to share the feelings of ___ the characters they portray.

    a. ( )
    b. { }
    c. [ ]
    d. " "

6. Choose the sentence below with the correct punctuation.

    a. Puzzled — Joe said, "You aren't going to pay me until ?"
    b. Puzzled, Joe said, "You aren't going to pay me until ?"
    c. Puzzled, Joe said, "You aren't going to pay me until —?"
    d. Puzzled, Joe said, "You aren't going to pay me until, ?"

7. Choose the sentence below with the correct punctuation.

    a. His employment wasn't consecutive, from 1999 to 2001 and 2002 – 2004.
    b. His employment wasn't consecutive, from 1999 – 2001 and 2002 – 2004.
    c. His employment wasn't consecutive, from 1999 _ 2001 and 2002_ 2004.
    d. His employment wasn't consecutive, from 1999, 2001 and 2002, 2004.

8. Choose the sentence below with the correct punctuation.

    a. Sandy asked for a one/third reduction on the cost of her damaged bag.

    b. Sandy asked for a one, third reduction on the cost of her damaged bag.

    c. Sandy asked for a one-third reduction on the cost of her damaged bag.

    d. None of the Above.

9. Choose the sentence below with the correct punctuation.

    a. Three minutes, two minutes, one minute

    b. Three minutes ... two minutes ... one minutes

    c. Three minutes - two minutes - one minutes

    d. None of the Above.

10. Choose the sentence below with the correct punctuation.

    a. Ms. Hermandez has offered to coach the basketball team, however, the competition is intense.

    b. Ms. Hermandez has offered to coach the basketball team, however the competition is intense.

    c. Ms. Hermandez has offered to coach the team; however, the competition is intense.

    d. None of the Above.

Directions: for questions 5 - 10 choose the sentence with the correct punctuation and capitalization.

11. Choose the sentence with the correct punctuation and capitalization.

a. The teacher just told us that it's time for the test.

b. Although his' car was fairly new he sold it to the banker.

c. She moved out of her parents' house into her's.

d. Who's brand new Camaro is this parked on the lawn?

12. Choose the sentence with the correct punctuation and capitalization.

a. I went to the supermarket: I bought chicken rice and fruits.

b. Iv'e never been this much in love before: until you.

c. I've just eaten these fruits; apples, peaches, plums and grapes.

d. The worst vices are: prostitution, gambling and drug trafficking.

13. Choose the sentence with the correct punctuation and capitalization.

a. The writer J. K. Rowling is British.

b. Have you seen my best Friend Scott who lives next door?

c. J. R. R. Tolkien, wrote the Lord of the Rings.

d. The US president, Barak Obama, arrived yesterday.

14. Choose the sentence with the correct punctuation and capitalization.

a. This video game is not interesting said Bobby to his friend.

b. This Video game is not interesting, said Bobby, to his friend.

c. "This video game is not interesting." Said Bobby to his friend.

d. "This video game is not interesting," said Bobby to his friend.

15. Choose the sentence with the correct punctuation and capitalization.

a. James Smith, the president of the club, invited the members to a party.

b. The president of the club James Smith, invited the members to a party.

c. The president of the club James Smith invited the members to a party.

d. James Smith the president of the club invited the members to a party.

16. Combine the following two sentences into one sentence with the same meaning.

Lisa applies herself to her studies.
Lisa may achieve excellent grades.

a. Lisa may achieve excellent grades in order to apply herself to her studies.

b. Provided that Lisa achieves good grades she may apply herself to her studies.

c. Lisa applies herself to her studies although she may achieve excellent grades.

d. Lisa may achieve excellent grades once she applies herself to her studies.

17. Combine the following two sentences into one sentence with the same meaning.

Richard took lessons in Spanish.
Richard wanted a job at the Spanish Embassy.

a. Richard took lessons in Spanish so that he wanted a job at the Spanish Embassy.

b. Richard took lessons in Spanish since he wanted a job at the Spanish Embassy.

c. Even if Richard wanted a job at the Spanish Embassy he took lessons in Spanish.

d. Having taken a job at the Spanish Embassy, Richard took lessons in Spanish.

18. Combine the following two sentences into one sentence with the same meaning.

The principal gives Bob a warning.
Bob does not disobey the rules.

a. Provided that the principal gives Bob a warning he does not disobey the rules.

b. Bob does not disobey the rules but also the principal gives him a warning

c. Even if the principal gives Bob a warning he does not disobey the rules.

d. The principal gives Bob a warning so that he does not disobey the rules.

19. Combine the following two sentences into one sentence with the same meaning.

Linda was very late for school.
Linda missed an important subject.

a. Because Linda missed an important subject she was very late for school.

b. Linda missed an important subject so that she was late for school.

c. Linda was so late for school that she missed an important subject.

d. Although Linda was very late for school, she missed an important subject.

20. Combine the following two sentences into one sentence with the same meaning.

Mary worked hard.

Mary succeeded at her job.

a. Mary succeeded at her job but she worked hard.

b. Whenever Mary succeeded at her job she worked hard.

c. Mary worked hard and thus she succeeded at her job.

d. However hard Mary worked, she succeeded at her job.

Directions: For questions 21 - 24 below, you are given a topic sentence. Choose the sentence which best develops the given topic sentence.

21. Education is the pathway out of poverty.

a. Getting a college education is very expensive.

b. Over a billion people worldwide earn less than a dollar a day.

c. Many children in poor countries do not have access to a good education.

d. Having a college degree results in more earning potential.

22. Parents should ensure their children's safety near water bodies.

a. Families should take trips to the beach together.

b. CPR is one of the most basic first aid skills.

c. Young children shouldn't be alone near water.

d. The earth is divided into four major oceans.

23. Couples should be properly prepared before having children.

a. China restricts the number of children a couple may have.

b. There are thousands of children in state care.

c. No contraceptive method is 100 percent safe.

d. The financial and emotional burden must be considered.

24. The TOEFL test is an adequate assessment of English proficiency.

a. Nonnative speakers usually find English difficult to learn.

b. English is one of the most widely spoken world languages.

c. American universities require non-natives to pass the TOEFL.

d. The four skill areas are assessed using varied methodology.

25. A college degree is an essential requirement for a well-paying job.

a. US and UK colleges are among the best in the world.

b. Some persons complain that their salaries are inadequate.

c. A high-school diploma only gives access to entry-level jobs.

d. Many foreign universities offer scholarships to Americans.

Questions 26 - 30 refer to the following passage.

Man has been observing the natural environment for ages and has been using principles learnt to advance and improve on various types of technology. The development of gliders is one (26) example. The evolution of gliders originated from man's fascination with bird flight. Gliders were developed after careful study of the flight pattern of birds. The first efforts to duplicate bird-like flying behavior happened from in the early 1800s. In Britain, Sir George Cayley, studying birds, in flight (27), attempted to understand the patterns observed and used the area of mathematics to formulate his observations. He was one of the first persons to formulate mathematical theories about flying. He theorized that the wings, when set at particular angles, caused the bird to ascend glide, or descend (28). From his observations and theories he designed a type of glider and tested its ability to remain in flight, successfully so.

In later years experimenters would come up with their own theories based on their observations and calculations. One sea captain, Jean Marie LeBris, kill an albatross (29) in order to study its wings and then designed and successfully flew what was later called the LeBris glider in 1857. A German, Otto Lilienthal, went even further. He covered peeled willow wands with waxed cotton cloth in his glider design. This design made several thousand flights, with constant improvements. The art of making gliders has been perfected (30) over the years. Gliders nowadays are able to fly for hundreds of miles.

Read the passage below and look at the numbered, underlined phrases. Choose the answer that is written correctly for each underlined part.

26. Choose the correct version.

   a. The development of Gliders is one

   b. The development of gliders are one

   c. The development of gliders is some

   d. Correct as is.

27. Choose the correct version.

   a. In Britain, Sir George Cayley, studying birds in flight

   b. In Britain; Sir George Cayley studying birds in flight

   c. In Britain Sir George Cayley, studying birds in flight

   d. Correct as is.

28. Choose the correct version.

    a. to ascend glide or descend

    b. to ascend, glide or descend

    c. to ascend, glide nor descend

    d. Correct as is.

29. Choose the correct version.

    a. One sea captain, Jean Marie LeBris, killed an albatross

    b. One sea captain – Jean Marie LeBris; kill an albatross

    c. One sea captain: Jean Marie LeBris: kills an albatross

    d. Correct as is.

30. Choose the correct version.

    a. have been perfected

    b. was been perfected

    c. has being perfected

    d. Correct as is.

Vocabulary

31. Because of its colorful fall _____, the maple is my favorite tree.

    a. Growth

    b. Branches

    c. Greenery

    d. Foliage

32. When Mr. Davis returned from southern Asia, he told us about the _____ that sometimes swept the area, bringing torrential rain.

    a. Monsoons

    b. Hurricanes

    c. Blizzards

    d. Floods

33. In heavily industrialized areas, the pollution of the air causes many to develop _____ diseases.

    a. Respiratory

    b. Cardiac

    c. Alimentary

    d. Circulatory

34. You can _____ some fires by covering them with dirt, while others require foam or water.

    a. Extinguish

    b. Distinguish

    c. Ignite

    d. Lessen

35. Through the use of powerful fans that circulate the heat over the food, _____ ovens work very efficiently.

    a. Microwave

    b. Broiler

    c. Convection

    d. Pressure

For questions 36 - 40, choose the word that best completes both sentences.

36. She always _____ people behind their back.
He _____ his opponents in his speeches.

    a. Offends

    b. Belittle

    c. Avoid

    d. Admire

37. They aren't exciting - all of the pictures are very _____.
His clothes are always very _____.

    a. Exciting

    b. Continuous

    c. Unforgiving

    d. Mundane

38. The auditorium was _____ when we arrived.
With 8 children, their house is always _____.

    a. Bedlam

    b. Placid

    c. Calm

    d. Noise

39. I would like to _____ if possible.
They tried, but couldn't _____ the disaster.

    a. Avert

    b. Promote

    c. Avenge

    d. Facilitate

40. **The water will soon _____.**
It is all gone. The water _____ over the last hour.

    a. Drip

    b. Dissipate

    c. Appear

    d. Degenerate

Answer Key

Reading

1. B
When someone is avid about something that means they are highly interested in the subject. The context clues are dull and boring, because they define the opposite of avid.

A is incorrect because dull and boring are not the opposite of good. C is incorrect because dull and boring are not the opposite of slow. D B. I = ?, r = 3%, t = 2 years, P = 6000. Convert rate to decimal. 3% = 0.03. Then plug in variables into the simple interest formula. I = P x r x t, I = 6000 x 0.03 x 2, I = $360 is incorrect because you can be a fast reader and still not be interested in what you have read.

2. A
The author is using a simile to compare the books to medicine. Medicine is what you take when you want to feel better. They are suggesting that if a person wants to feel good, they should read Dr. Seuss' books.

Option B is incorrect because there is no mention of a doctor's office. Option C is incorrect because it is using the literal meaning of medicine and the author is using medicine in a figurative way. Option D is incorrect because it makes no sense. We know not to eat books.

3. D
The publisher is described as intelligent because he knew to get in touch with a famous author in order to develop a book that children would be interested in reading.

Option A is incorrect because we can assume that all book publishers must know how to read. Option B is incorrect because it says in the article that more than one publisher was concerned about whether or not children liked to read. Option D is incorrect because there is no mention in the article about how well The Cat in the Hat sold when it was first published.

4. B
The passage describes in detail how Dr. Seuss had a great effect on the lives of children through his writing. It names several of his books, tells how he helped children become avid readers and explains his style of writing.

Option A is incorrect because that is just one single fact about the passage. Option C is incorrect because that is just one single fact about the passage. Option D is incorrect because that is just one single fact about the passage. Again, Option B is correct because it encompasses ALL the facts in the passage, not just one single fact.

5. A
Low blood sugar occurs both in diabetics and healthy adults.

6. B
None of the statements are the author's opinion.

7. A
The author's purpose is to inform.

8. A
The only statement that is not a detail is, "A doctor can diagnosis this medical condition by asking the patient questions and testing."

9. A
We know that an annex is like an attic because the text states the annex was above Otto Frank's building.

Option B is incorrect because an office building doesn't have bedrooms. Option C is incorrect because a basement would be below the office building. Option D is incorrect because there would not be a kitchen in an office building.

10. B
The diary has been published in 55 languages so people all over the world can learn about Anne. That is why the passage says it has been continuously in print.

Option A is incorrect because it is too vague. Option C is incorrect because it was published after Anne died and she did not write in all three languages. Option D is incorrect because the passage does not give us any information about what languages Otto Frank spoke.

11. C

You use process of elimination to figure this out.

Option A cannot be the correct answer because otherwise the passage would have simply said that Anne and Margot both died of starvation. Options B and D cannot be correct because if the Germans had done something specifically to murder Anne, the passage would have stated that directly. By the process of elimination, Option C has to be the correct answer.

12. D

We can figure this out using context clues. The paragraph is talking about Anne's diary and so, outlet in this instance is a place where Anne can pour her feelings.

Option A is incorrect answer. That is the literal meaning of the word outlet and the passage is using the figurative meaning. Option B is incorrect because that is the secondary literal meaning of the word outlet, as in an outlet mall. Again, we are looking for figurative meaning. Option C is incorrect because there are no clues in the text to support that answer.

13. B

This passage describes the different categories for traditional stories. The other options are facts from the passage, not the main idea of the passage. The main idea of a passage will always be the most general statement. For example, Option A, Myths, fables, and folktales are not the same thing, and each describes a specific type of story. This is a true statement from the passage, but not the main idea of the passage, since the passage also talks about how some cultures may classify a story as a myth and others as a folktale.

The statement, from Option B, Traditional stories can be categorized in different ways by different people, is a more general statement that describes the passage.

14. B
Option B is the best choice, categories that group traditional stories according to certain characteristics.

Options A and C are false and can be eliminated right away. Option D is designed to confuse. Option D may be true, but it is not mentioned in the passage.

15. D
The best answer is Option D, traditional stories themselves are a part of the larger category of folklore, which may also include costumes, gestures, and music.

All of the other options are false. Traditional stories are part of the larger category of Folklore, which includes other things, not the other way around.

16. A
There is a distinct difference between a myth and a legend, although both are folktales.

17. B
The correct answer can be found in the fourth sentence of the first paragraph.

Option A is incorrect because repenting begins the day AFTER Mardi Gras. Option C is incorrect because you can celebrate Mardi Gras without being a member of a Krewe.

Option D is incorrect because exploration does not play any role in a modern Mardi Gras celebration.

18. A
The second sentence is the last paragraph states that Krewes are led by the Kings and Queens. Therefore, you must have to be part of a Krewe to be its King or its Queen.

Option B is incorrect because it never states in the passage that only people from France can be Kings and Queen of Mardi Gras. Option C is incorrect because the passage says nothing about having to speak French. Option D is incorrect because the passage does state that the Kings and Queens throw doubloons, which is fake money.

19. C

The first sentences of BOTH the 2nd and 3rd paragraphs mention that French explorers started this tradition in New Orleans.

Options A, B and D are incorrect because they are just names of cities or countries listed in the 2nd paragraph.

20. B

In the final paragraph the word spectator is used to describe people who are watching the parade and catching cups, beads and doubloons. A and C are incorrect because we know the people who participate are part of Krewes. People who work the floats and parades are also part of Krewes

D is incorrect because the passage makes no mention of people who do not celebrate Mardi Gras.

21. B

All thunderstorms will go through three stages. This is taken directly from the text, "All thunderstorms, regardless of type, go through three stages: the cumulus stage, the mature stage, and the dissipation stage."

22. A

The correct order of the process is seen in this passage:

"Clouds form as warm air carrying moisture rises. As the warm air rises, it cools. The moist water vapor begins to condense as the temperature cools. This releases energy that keeps the air warmer than its surroundings. The result is that it continues to rise."

23. A

Helen's parents hired Anne to teach Helen to communicate.

Option B is incorrect because the passage states Anne had trouble finding her way around, which means she could walk. Option C is incorrect because you don't hire a teacher to teach someone to play. Option D is incorrect because by age 6, if Helen had never eaten, she would have starved to death.

24. B

The correct answer because that fact is stated directly in the passage. The passage explains that Anne taught Helen to hear by allowing her to feel the vibrations in her throat.

25. A
We can infer that Anne is a patient teacher because she did not leave or lose her temper when Helen bit or hit her; she just kept trying to teach Helen.

Option B is incorrect because Anne taught Helen to read and talk. Option C is incorrect because Anne could hear. She was partially blind, not deaf. Option D is incorrect because it does not have to do with patience.

Computational Mathematics

1. C
8974 – 8256 = 718

2. A
4404 / 8 = 550.5

3. D
274 * 139 = 38086

4. B
3567 + 99 = 3666

5. A
2 + a number divided by 7.
(2 + X) divided by 7.
(2 + X)/7

6. A
60/x = 75/100
60 * 100/X = 75
6000/75 = X
X = 80

7. C
71 ÷ 1000 = 0.071.

8. A
.33 × .59 = .195

9. A
Collect like terms, 7x = 47 + 9 = 56,
divide both sides by 7
x = 8

10. C
The ten thousandths place in 1.7389 will be the 4th decimal place, 9.

11. A
.87 - .48 = 0.39.

12. C
Forty nine thousandths will place the '9' in the 3rd decimal place, 0.049.

13. D
a. 3/4 * 2/2 = 6/8
b. 3/4 * 3/3 = 9/12
c. 3/4 * 4/4 = 12/18 – Incorrect!
d. 3/4 * 7/7 = 21/28

14. D
a. 84/231 = 12/33 > 1/3
b. 6/35 = 1/5 < 1/3
c. 3/22 = 1/7 < 1/3
d. b and c are less than 1/3

15. C
Here are the options:
a. 1
b. $\sqrt{2}$ = 1.414
c. 3/2 = 1.5   Largest number
d. 4/3 = 1.33

16. B
Collecting similar terms (algebraic addition).
2b + 9b – 5b = 11b - 5b = 6b

17. C
4.7 + .9 + .01 = 5.61.

18. D
60/100 = 12/X
60 = 12 * 100/X
60X = 1200
X = 1200/60
X = 20.

19. D
.84/.7 = 1.2

20. C
4120 − 3216 = 904

21. D
2417 + 1004 = 3421

22. B
0.12 + 2/5 + 3/5, Convert decimal to fraction to get 3/25 + 2/5 + 3/5, = (3 + 10 + 15)/25, = 28/25 = 1 3/25

23. D
700,653 − 70,099 = 630,0554

24. A
0.25 + 2 1/3 + 2/3, first convert decimal to fraction, 1/4 + 1/3 + 2/3, (3 + 4 + 8)/12, = 15/12 = 5/4 = 1 1/4

25. B
10% of 300 = 30 and 50% of 20 = 10 so 30 + 10 = 40.

Applied Mathematics

1. C
1 hour is equal to 3600 seconds and 1 kilometer is equal to 1000 meters. So at 72 k/hr, the train covers 72,000 meters in 36,000 seconds. Distance covered in 12 seconds = 12 × 72,000/3,600 = 240 meters.

2. B

Volume = Volume of large cylinder - Volume of small cylinder
(Volume of cylinder = area of base x height)
Volume = (π 12^2 x 10) - (π 6^2 x 5), 1440π - 180π
Volume = 1260π in^3

3. A

After breakage, the total number of eggs that Tony sold
= 12×15 – 16 = 164. Total amount for selling 164 eggs =
164×0.54 = $89.1.
Percentage profit = (89.1 – 80) × 100/80 = 11.25%

4. B

Absent students = 83 – 72 = 11
Percent of absent students =   11/83 X 100 = 13.25
Round to 13%.

5. A

P = 200, r = 15%, I = 245 – 200 = $45, t =? First convert the
rate to a decimal, 15% = 0.15. I = P x r x t. Therefore, 45 =
200 x 0.15 x t, 45 = 30t, t = 45/30 = 1.5. She will have to
wait for 1½ years for his $200 to earn $45 interest to become $245.

6. C

I = 600, r = 3, t = 2 and P = ? Using the formula, P = 100 x
interest/ r x t

100 x 600/ 3 x 2 = 60000/6 = 10,000. The original amount
deposited was $10,000

7. B

Based on this graph, a person that is 85 or older will make
31.3 visits to the hospital every year.

8. A

Based on this graph, the number of visits per year is going
up as age goes up, so we can expect a person that is 95 to
have more than 31.3 visits to the hospital each year.

9. A

The formula of the volume of cylinder is = $\prod$ r^2h. Where $\prod$
is 3.142, r is radius of the cross sectional area, and h is the
height. So the volume will be = 3.142 × 2.5^2 ×12 =   235.65
m^3.

10. C
Large cube is made up of 8 smaller cubes with 5 cm sides.
Volume = Volume of small cube x 8
Volume = (5 x 5 x 5) x 8, 125 x 8
Volume = 1000 cm^3

11. A
The line is pointing towards numbers greater than 2. The equation is therefore, X > 2.

12. C
Pythagorean Theorem:
(Hypotenuse)^2 = (Perpendicular)^2 + (Base)^2
$h^2 = a^2 + b^2$

Given: a = 6, h = 10
$h^2 = a^2 + b^2$
$b^2 = h^2 - a^2$
$b^2 = 10^2 + 6^2$
$b^2 = 100 - 36$
$b^2 = 64$
$b = 8$

13. D
Two parallel lines intersected by a third line with angles of 75°
x = 75° (corresponding angles)
x + y = 180° (supplementary angles)
y = 180° - 75°
y = 105°

14. D
Two parallel lines (*m* & side AB) intersected by side AC.
Angle A = angle a, (interior angles) so a = 50°

15. D
Circle with diameter and a square within the circle
Area of circle = π x r^2
Area of circle = π x 4^2
Area of circle = 16 π cm^2

16. B
Perimeter of a parallelogram is the sum of the sides.
Perimeter = 2(l + b)
Perimeter = 2(3 +10), 2 x 13
Perimeter = 26 cm.

17. C
87% = 87/100 = 0.87

18. C
Volume of a cylinder is π x r^2 x h
Diameter = 5 ft. so radius is 2.5 ft.
Volume of cylinder= π x 2.5^2 x 2
= π x 6.25 x 2 = 12.5 π
Approximate π to 3.142
Volume of the cylinder = 39.25

Volume of a rectangle = height X width X length.
= 5 X 5 X 4 = 100

Total volume = Volume of rectangular solid + volume of cylinder
Total volume = 100 + 39.25
Total volume = 139.25 ft^3 or approximately 140 ft^3

19. D
The jacket costs $545.00 so we can round up to $550. 10% of $550 is 55. We can round down to $50, which is easier to work with. $550 - $50 is $500. The jacket will cost about $500.

The actual cost will be 10% X 545 = $54.50
545 – 54.50 = $490.50

20. C
Pythagorean Theorem:
$(Hypotenuse)^2$ = $(Perpendicular)^2$ + $(Base)^2$
$h^2 = a^2 + b^2$

Given: $h^2 = 3^2 + 4^2$
$h^2 = \sqrt{25}$
h = 5

21. D
P= $5,500, t = 3 years, r = 5%, I = ? convert rate to decimal and 5% = 0.05
I = 5,500 x 0.05 x 3 = 825. Total amount in the account = principal + interest or 5,500 + 825 = $6,325

22. D
First calculate total square feet, which is 15 X 24 = 360 sq. ft. Next convert to square yards, (1sq. ft. = 0.1111 sq. yards) which is 360 X 0.1111 = 39.9999 or 40 square yards. At $0.50 per square yard, the total cost is $20.

23. B
Flat Screen TVs are the third best-selling product.

24. B
The two products that are closest in the number of sales, are Flat Screen TVs and Radar Detectors.

25. B
I = ?, r = 3%, t = 2 years, P = 6000. Convert rate to decimal. 3% = 0.03. Then plug in variables into the simple interest formula. I = P x r x t, I = 6000 x 0.03 x 2, I = $360.

Language

1. B
A colon is used before a list of items following an independent clause.

2. A
A comma is used to introduce short quotations or proverbs.

3. A
The colon is used in the salutation of a formal business letter.

4. B
An apostrophe is placed before the letter "s" to indicate singular possession.

5. A
A parenthesis is used to set off asides and explanations only

when the material is not essential or when it consists of one or more sentences.

6. C

The dash is used when the speaker cannot continue.

7. B

The dash is used to indicate a closed range of values.

8. C

A hyphen is used with fractions used as adjectives.

9. B

Ellipsis (...) is used to indicate passage of time.

10. A

"However" generally has a comma before and after.

11. A

Option A uses the apostrophe correctly in "it's." All of the other options have incorrect apostrophe use.

12. A

Option A uses the colon correctly. Option B use the incorrect form, "Iv'e." Option C uses a semicolon instead of a colon. Option D uses the colon incorrectly.

13. A

Option A has correct punctuation and capitalization. Option B incorrectly capitalizes "friend." Option C uses a comma incorrectly. In option D, "president" should be capitalized .

14. D

Option A is incorrect because it does not use quotation marks. Option B does not use quotation marks and incorrectly places a comma after Bobby. Option C incorrectly places a period after Bobby.

15. A

Option A is the only option which uses the comma correctly.

16. D
17. B
18. D

19. C
20. C
21. D
22. C
23. D
24. D
25. C

26. D
The phrase is correct as is. Option A incorrectly capitalizes "gliders." Option B incorrectly uses "are." Option C incorrectly uses "some."

27. A
Option A uses commas correctly. Option B incorrectly uses a semi colon instead of a comma. Option C omits a comma after "Britain."

28. B
Option B is the only option that uses commas correctly.

29. A
Option A uses commas correctly. Option B uses the dash where it is not needed, and a semi colon instead of a comma. Option C uses colons instead of comma.

30. D
The phrase is correct as is, and uses the past perfect correctly. The other options all use the past perfect incorrectly.

Vocabulary

31. D
Foliage: plant leaves

32. A
Monsoons: a seasonal prevailing wind in the region of South and Southeast Asia, blowing from the southwest between May and September and bringing rain

33. A

Respiratory: of, relating to, or affecting respiration or the organs of respiration.

34. A
Extinguish: cause (a fire or light) to cease to burn or shine.
35. C
Convection: the movement caused within a fluid by the tendency of hotter and therefore less dense material to rise, and colder, denser material to sink under the influence of gravity, which consequently results in transfer of heat.

36. B
Belittle: make (someone or something) seem unimportant.

37. D
Mundane: Ordinary; not new.

38. A
Bedlam: A place or situation of chaotic uproar, and where confusion prevails.

39. A
Avert: To ward off, or prevent, the occurrence or effects of.

40. B
Dissipate: disperse or scatter.

Conclusion

CONGRATULATIONS! You have made it this far because you have applied yourself diligently to practicing for the exam and no doubt improved your potential score considerably! Getting into a good school is a huge step in a journey that might be challenging at times but will be many times more rewarding and fulfilling. That is why being prepared is so important.

Study then Practice and then Succeed!

Good Luck!

FREE Ebook Version

Download a FREE Ebook version of the publication!

Suitable for tablets, iPad, iPhone, or any smart phone.

Go to
http://tinyurl.com/o3xqnvn

TABE Test Strategy!

Learn to increase your score using time-tested secrets for answering multiple choice questions!

This practice book has everything you need to know about answering multiple choice questions on the TABE!

You will learn 12 strategies for answering multiple choice questions and then practice each strategy with over 45 reading comprehension multiple choice questions, with extensive commentary from exam experts!

Also included are strategies and practice questions for basic math, plus math tips, tricks and shortcuts!

Maybe you have read this kind of thing before, and maybe feel you don't need it, and you are not sure if you are going to buy this Book.

Remember though, it only a few percentage points divide the PASS from the FAIL students.

Even if our multiple choice strategies increase your score by a few percentage points, isn't that worth it?

Get Organized, Study Less and Get Higher Marks!

Here is what you will learn:

- How to Organize your Study Space

- Four different strategies for taking notes

- Reading strategies for textbooks, essays, novels and literature

- How to Concentrate - What is concentration and how do you do it!

- Using Flash Cards - Complete guide to using flash cards including the Leitner method.

and LOT more... Including time management, sleep, nutrition, motivation, brain food, procrastination, study schedules and more!

https://www.createspace.com/4060298

Enter Code LYFZGQB5 for 25% off!

Endnotes

Reading comprehension passages where noted below are used under the Creative Commons Attribution-ShareAlike 3.0 License

http://en.wikipedia.org/wiki/Wikipedia:Text_of_Creative_ Commons_Attribution-ShareAlike_3.0_Unported_License

[1] Immune System. In *Wikipedia*. Retrieved November 12, 2010 from, en.wikipedia.org/wiki/Immune_system.

[2] White Blood Cell. In *Wikipedia*. Retrieved November 12, 2010 from en.wikipedia.org/wiki/White_blood_cell.

[3] Infectious disease. In *Wikipedia*. Retrieved November 12, 2010 from http://en.wikipedia.org/wiki/Infectious_disease.

[4] Thunderstorm. In *Wikipedia*. Retrieved November 12, 2010 from en.wikipedia.org/wiki/Thunderstorm.

[5] Meteorology. In *Wikipedia*. Retrieved November 12, 2010 from en.wikipedia.org/wiki/Outline_of_meteorology.

[6] U.S. Navy Seal. In *Wikipedia*. Retrieved November 12, 2010 from en.wikipedia.org/wiki/United_States_Navy_ SEALs.

[7] Mythology. In *Wikipedia*. Retrieved November 12, 2010 from en.wikipedia.org/wiki/Mythology.

Made in the USA
Middletown, DE
16 May 2016